THINGS I'VE SAID TO MY CHILDREN

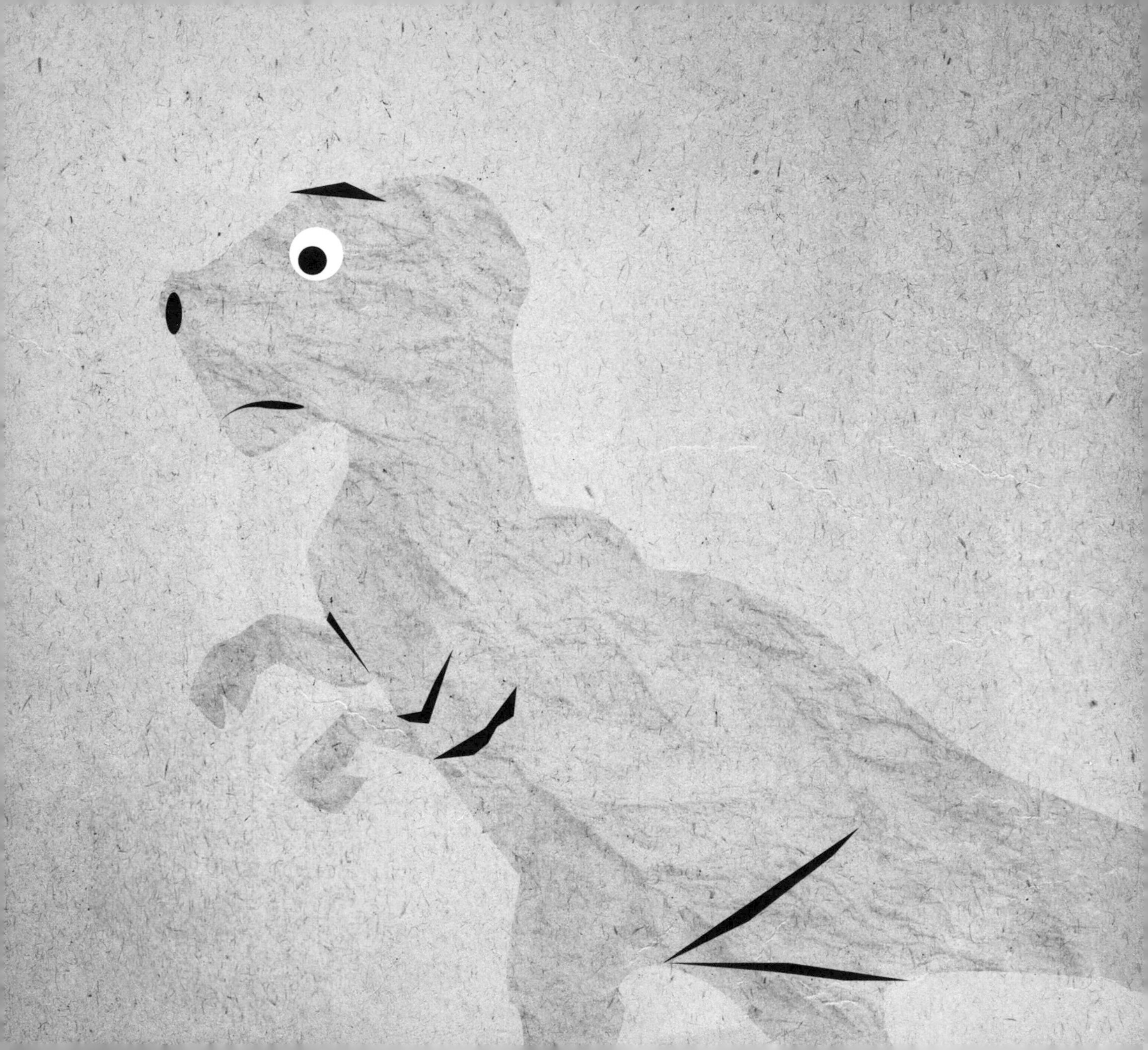

THINGS I'VE SAID TO MY CHILDREN

NATHAN RIPPERGER

TEN SPEED PRESS
Berkeley

Copyright © 2015 by Nathan Ripperger

All rights reserved.
Published in the United States by Ten Speed Press, an imprint of the
Crown Publishing Group, a division of Penguin Random House LLC, New York.
www.crownpublishing.com
www.tenspeed.com

Ten Speed Press and the Ten Speed Press colophon are registered
trademarks of Penguin Random House LLC.

Library of Congress Cataloging-in-Publication Data
Ripperger, Nathan.
  Things I've said to my children / Nathan Ripperger. — First edition.
      pages cm
1. Child rearing—Humor. 2. Parenting—Humor. 3. Children—Humor. I. Title.
  PN6231.C315.R57 2015
  818'.5407—dc23
                    2015005187

Hardcover ISBN: 978-1-60774-830-4
eBook ISBN: 978-1-60774-831-1

Printed in China

Design by Chloe Rawlins
Cover and interior illustrations by Nathan Ripperger

10 9 8 7 6 5 4 3 2 1

First Edition

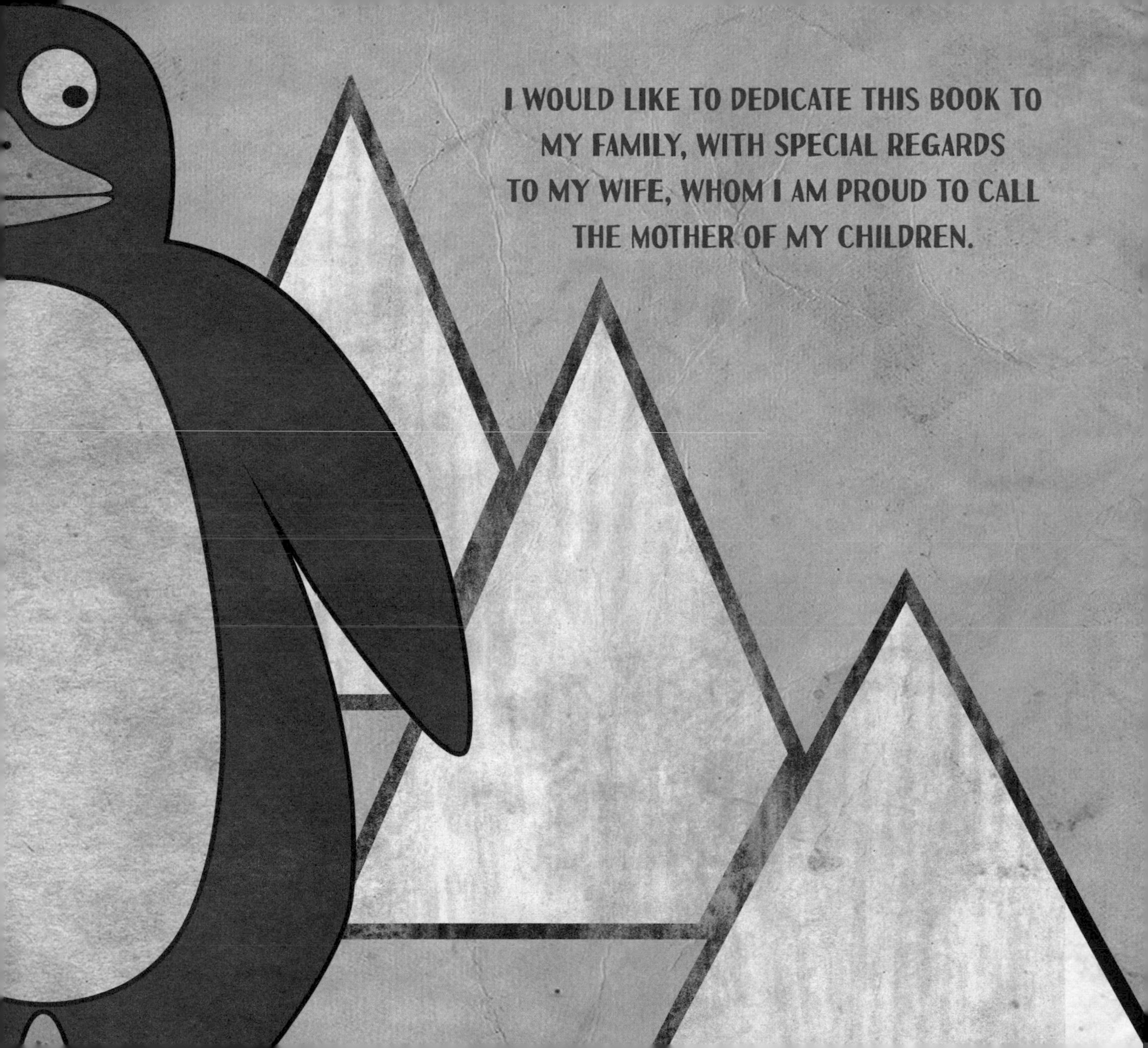

I WOULD LIKE TO DEDICATE THIS BOOK TO MY FAMILY, WITH SPECIAL REGARDS TO MY WIFE, WHOM I AM PROUD TO CALL THE MOTHER OF MY CHILDREN.

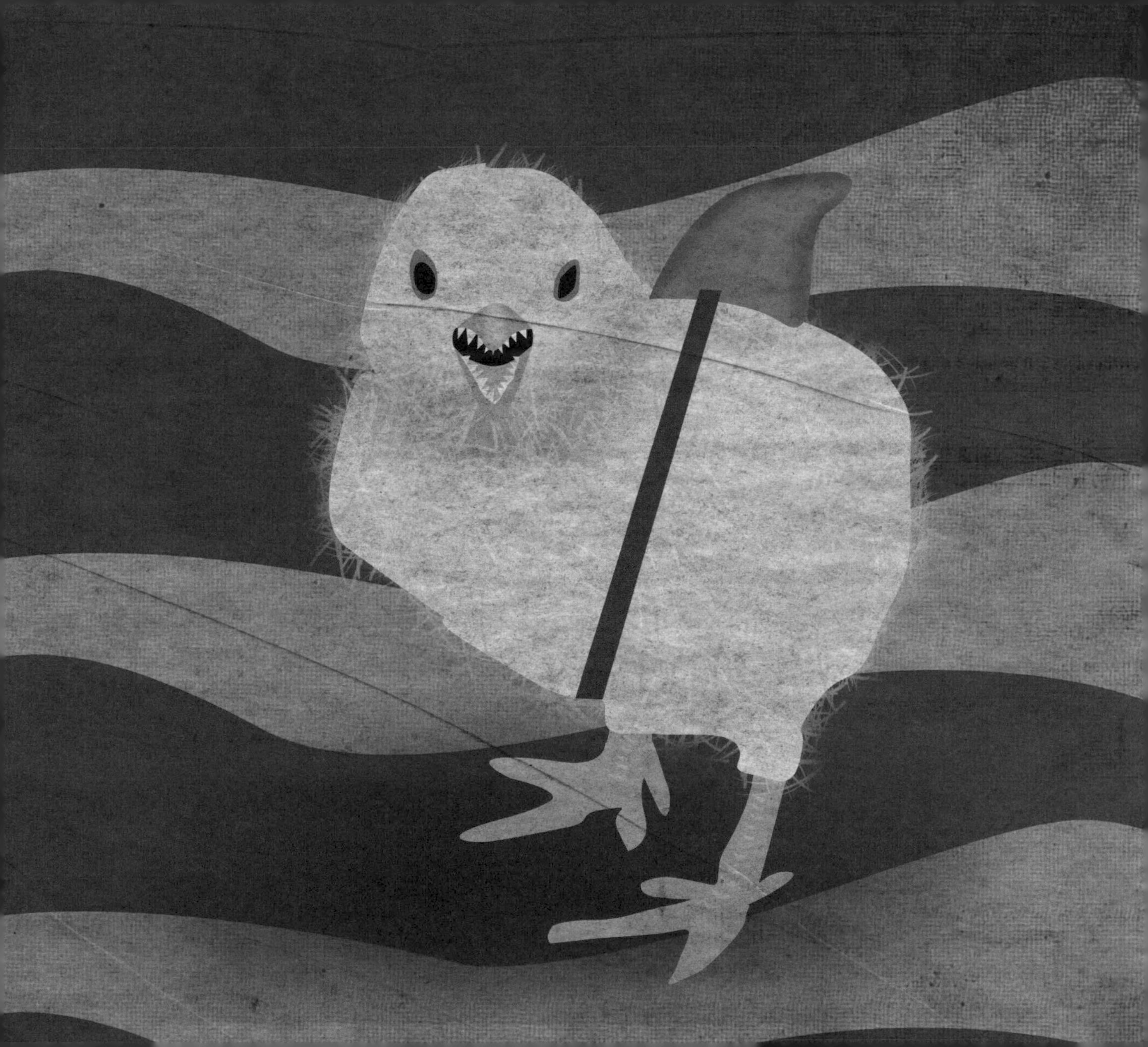

INTRODUCTION

Children are odd creatures. They are human tornadoes of irrationality and ridiculousness. And it's our job as a parents to deal with them. At times, parenting is the definition of absurdity. The things that find their way into children's mouths and the places their hands make their way into are beyond the imagination of most people. Since becoming a parent, on several occasions I have found myself saying things that I was sure that no other person in the history of humanity had uttered. These phrases stood out to me and I decided to commemorate their strangeness in graphic designs. Thus the birth of *Things I've Said to My Children*.

We want our children to be "normal." We would love to go through a grocery store without our children dancing with the bread or licking the grocery carts. (Or at least I hope it's not only my children that lick everything.) It seems that sometimes the only things that leave our mouths are longs lists of *Don'ts*, *Stops*, and *Nos*. If that's how you feel, rest assured, you are not alone!

This book stands as a testament to the solidarity of parenthood. This collection of phrases that I have curated from many of my own experiences and from parents around the United States and the world shows how not alone we are as we deal with our own little tornadoes. As you look through this book, I'm sure that you will come across phrases that mirror some you've said yourself. Honestly, I'm surprised how many people have told me they have also said the exact phrase, "I'm not talking to you until you are wearing underwear."

As a father of five children, including a new baby, I'm sure I will say many more odd things to my kids in the future. However, as my four oldest boys have grown, the absurdity has diminished. I don't dwell too much on the lack of random things my ten-year-old puts in his mouth, but I do look forward to the whimsical yet erratic behavior of the toddler waiting in the wings. So embrace the absurdity, love your little tornadoes as they are, and enjoy the things you say to your children.

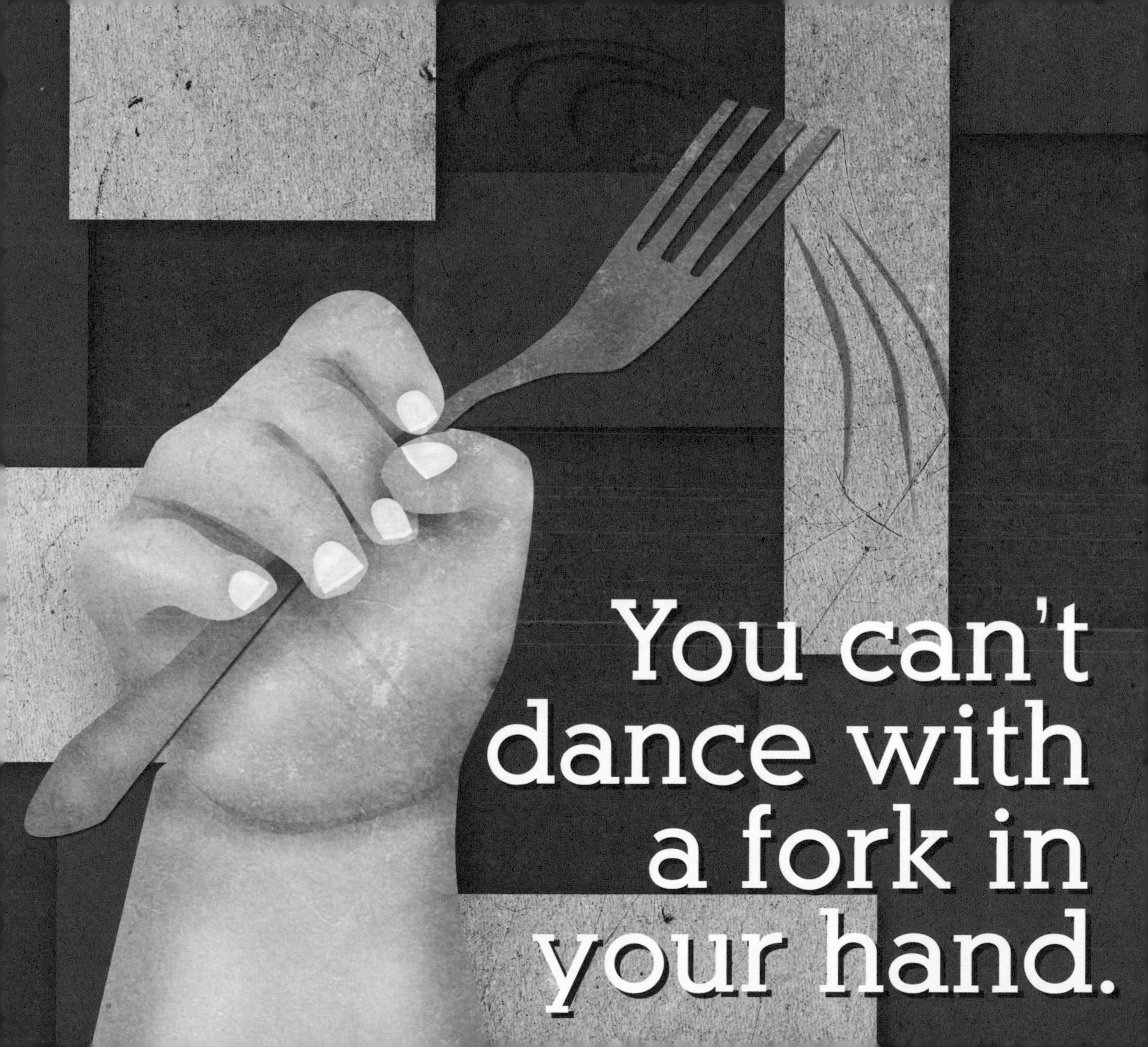
You can't dance with a fork in your hand.

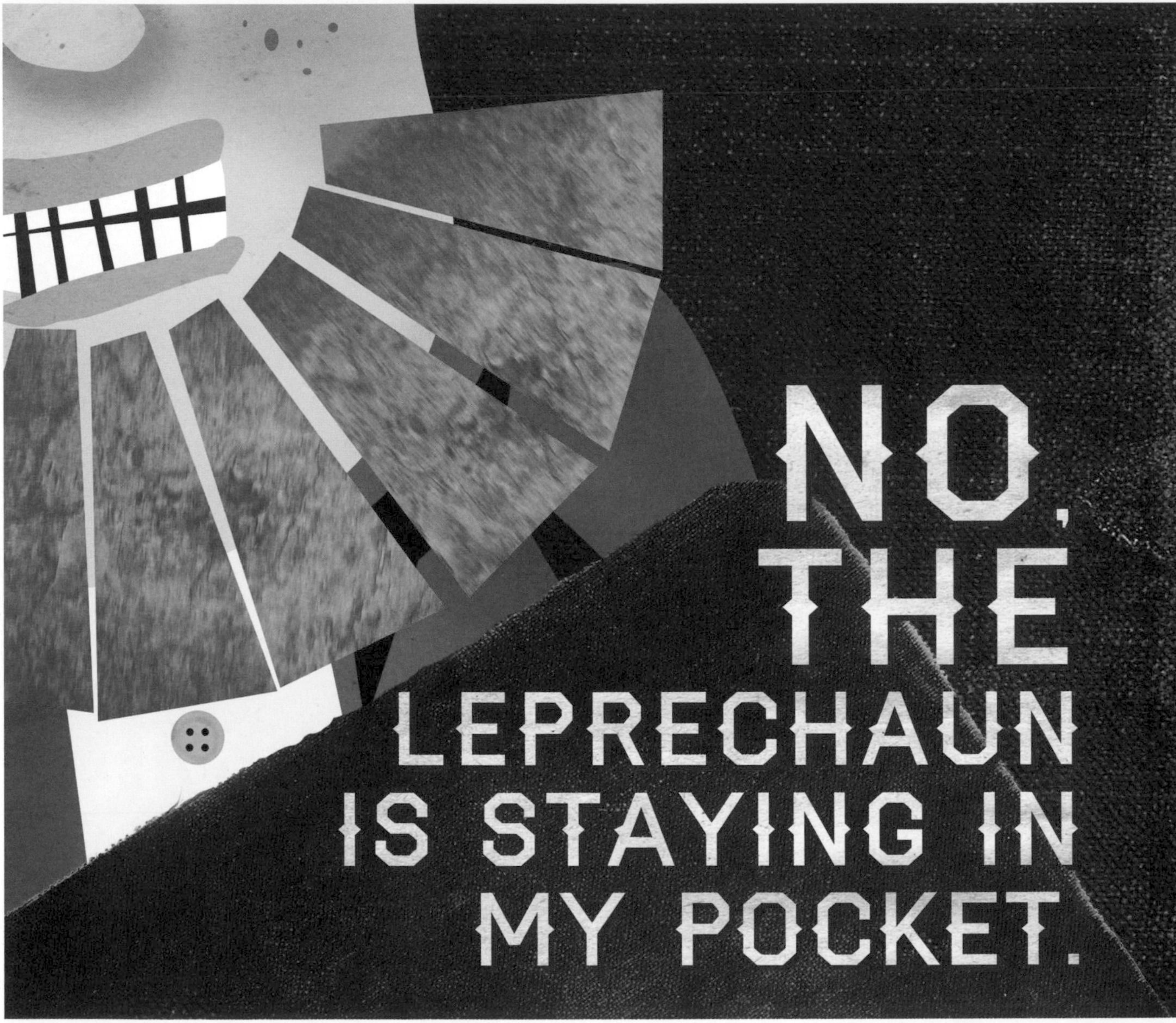

NO, THE LEPRECHAUN IS STAYING IN MY POCKET.

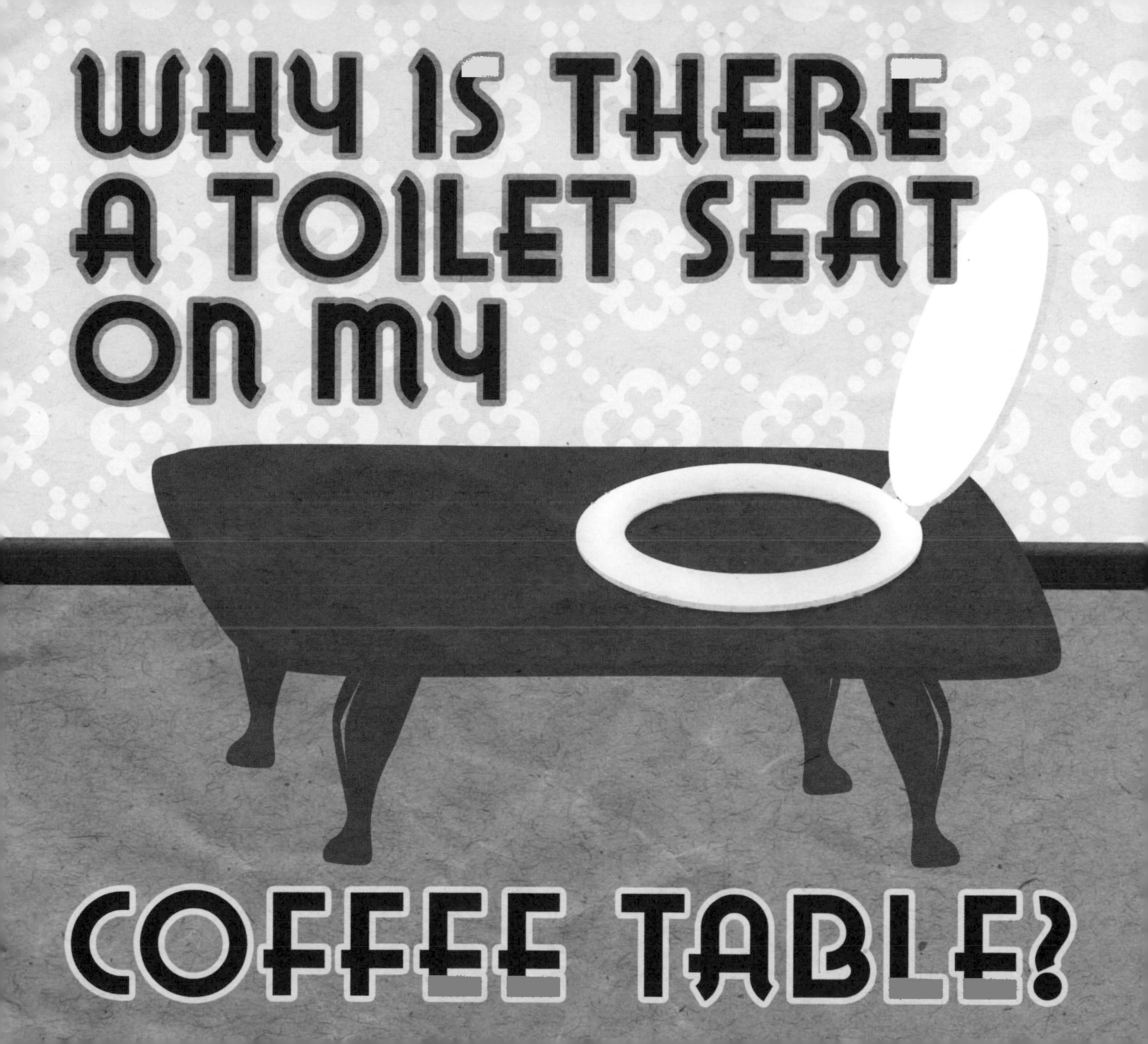
WHY IS THERE
A TOILET SEAT
ON MY
COFFEE TABLE?

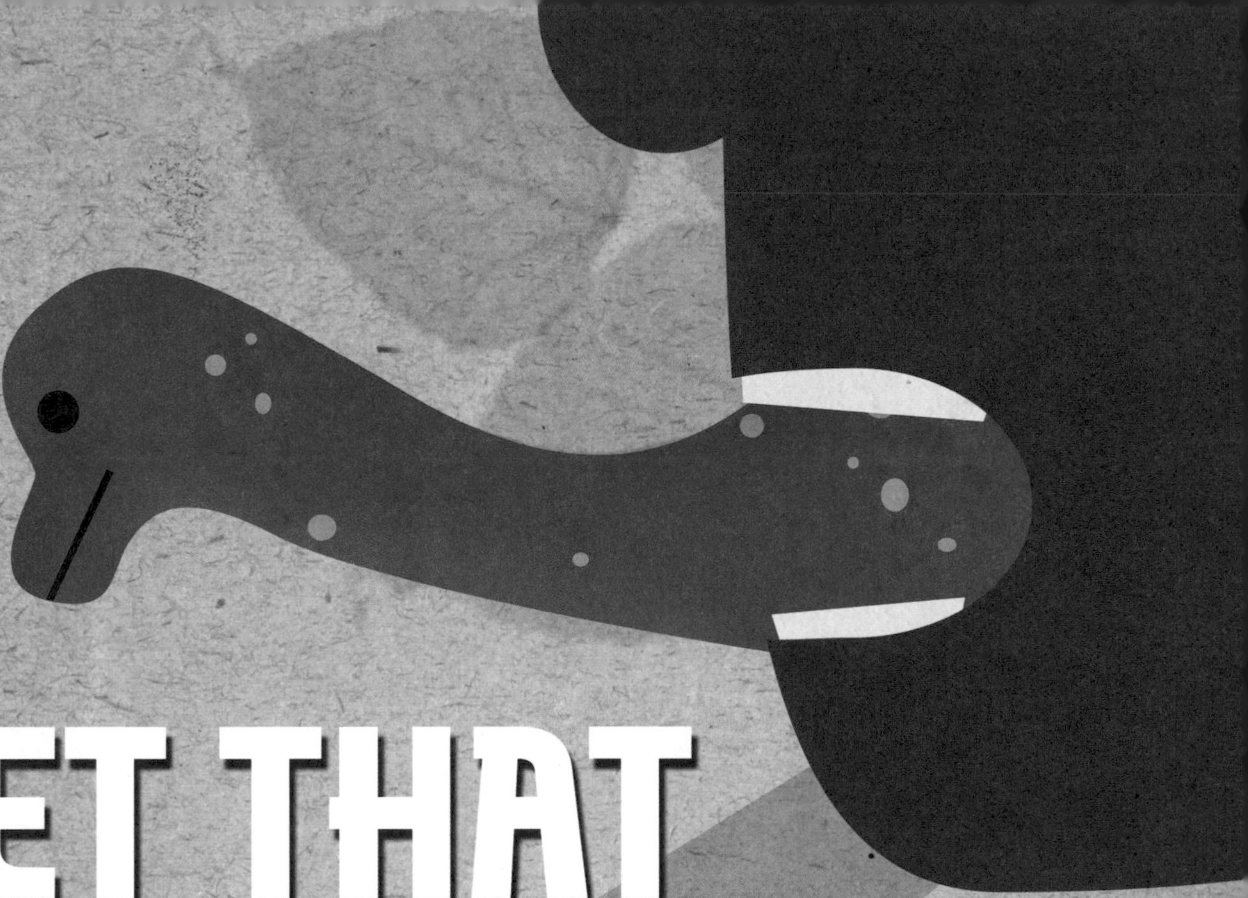

GET THAT DINOSAUR OUT OF YOUR MOUTH.

DON'T BITE THE LAMP SHADE.

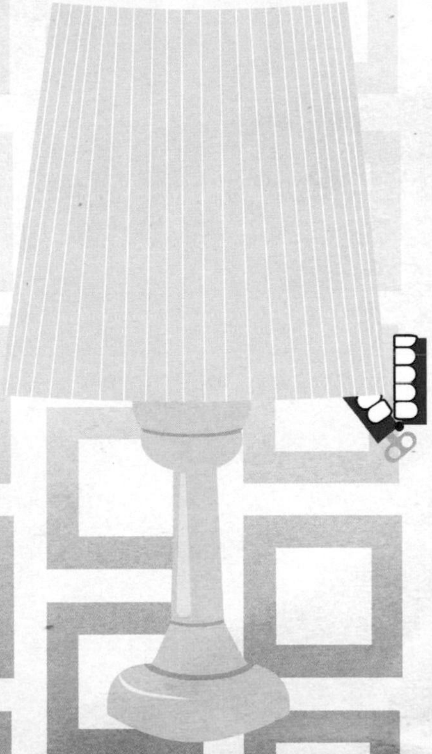

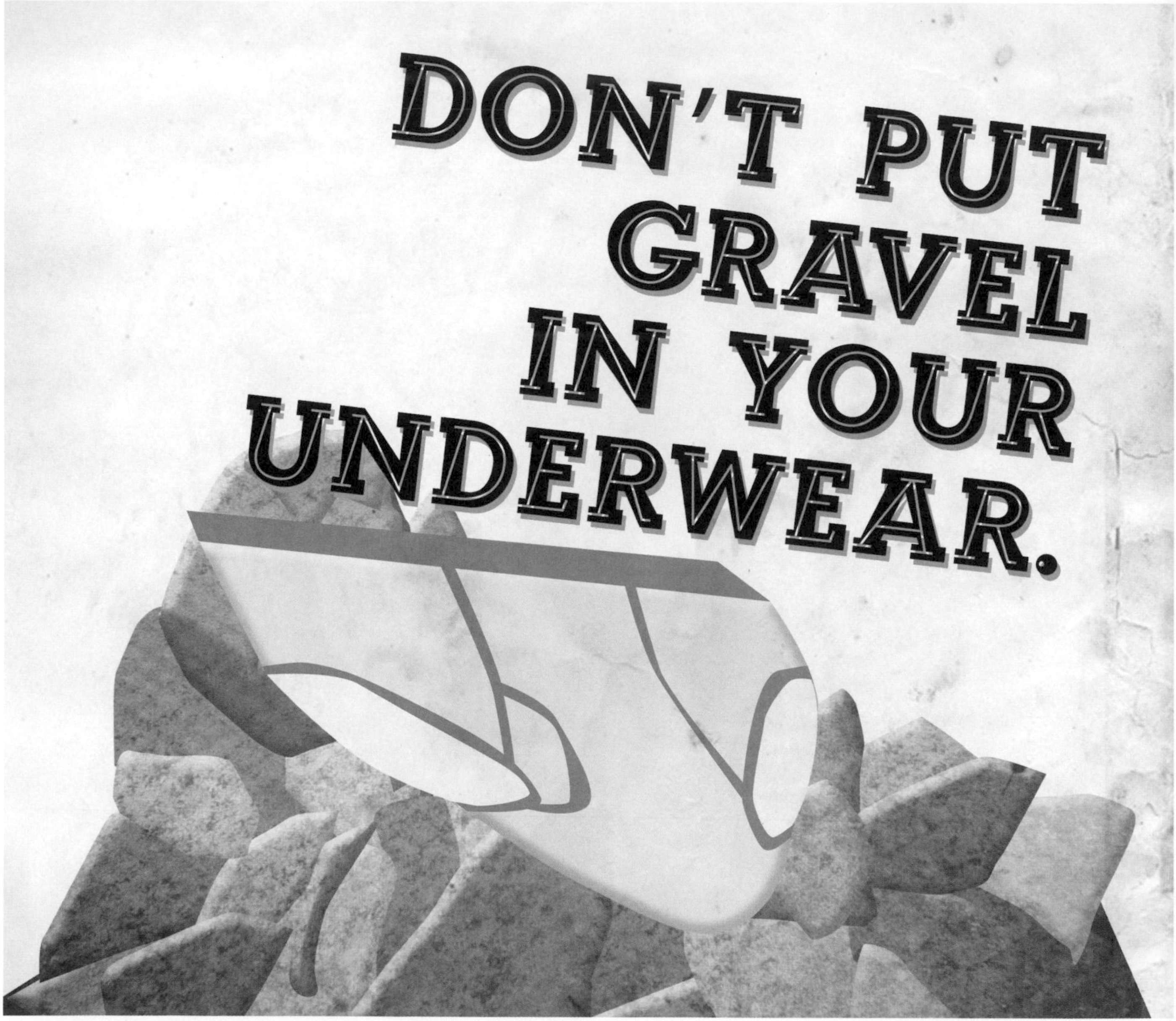
DON'T PUT GRAVEL IN YOUR UNDERWEAR.

STOP RIDING THE CHRISTMAS TREE LIKE A HORSE.

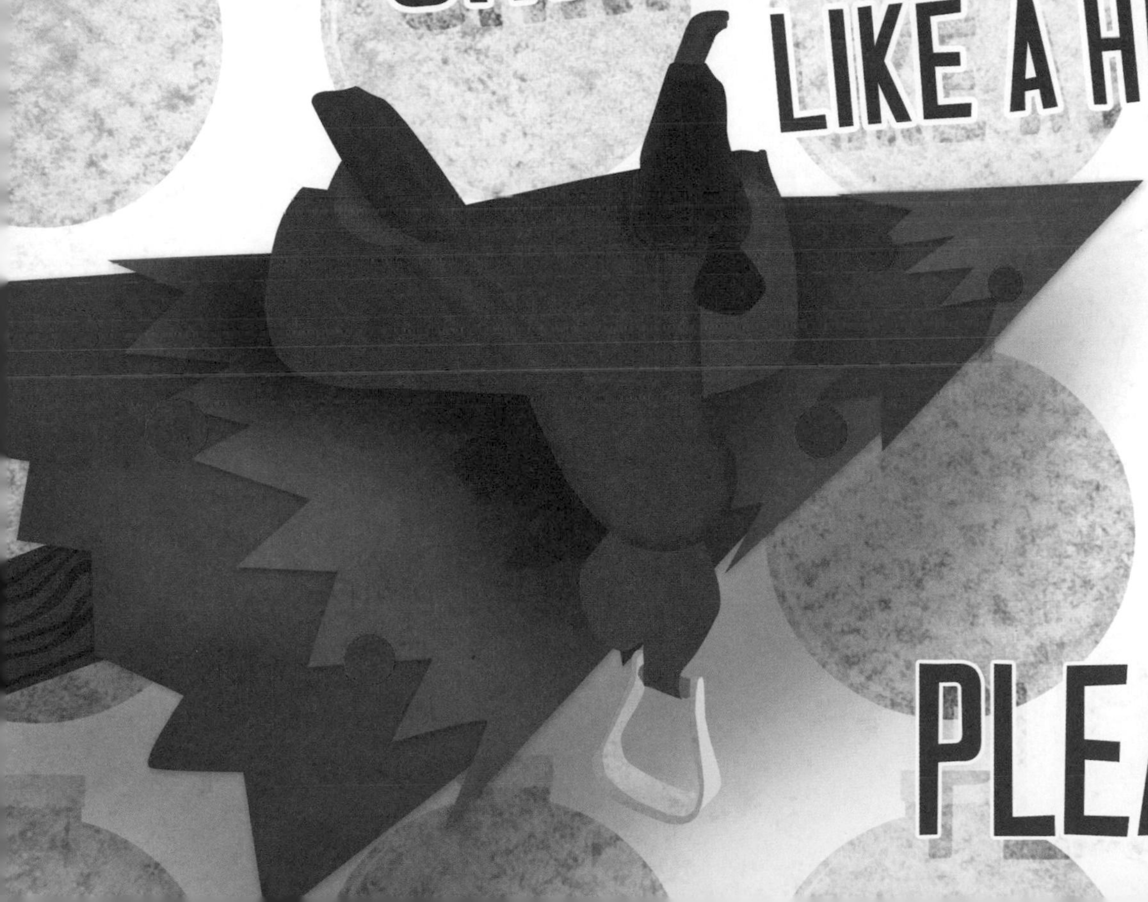

PLEASE?

Please don't **FREAK OUT** because you have a mustache on your foot.

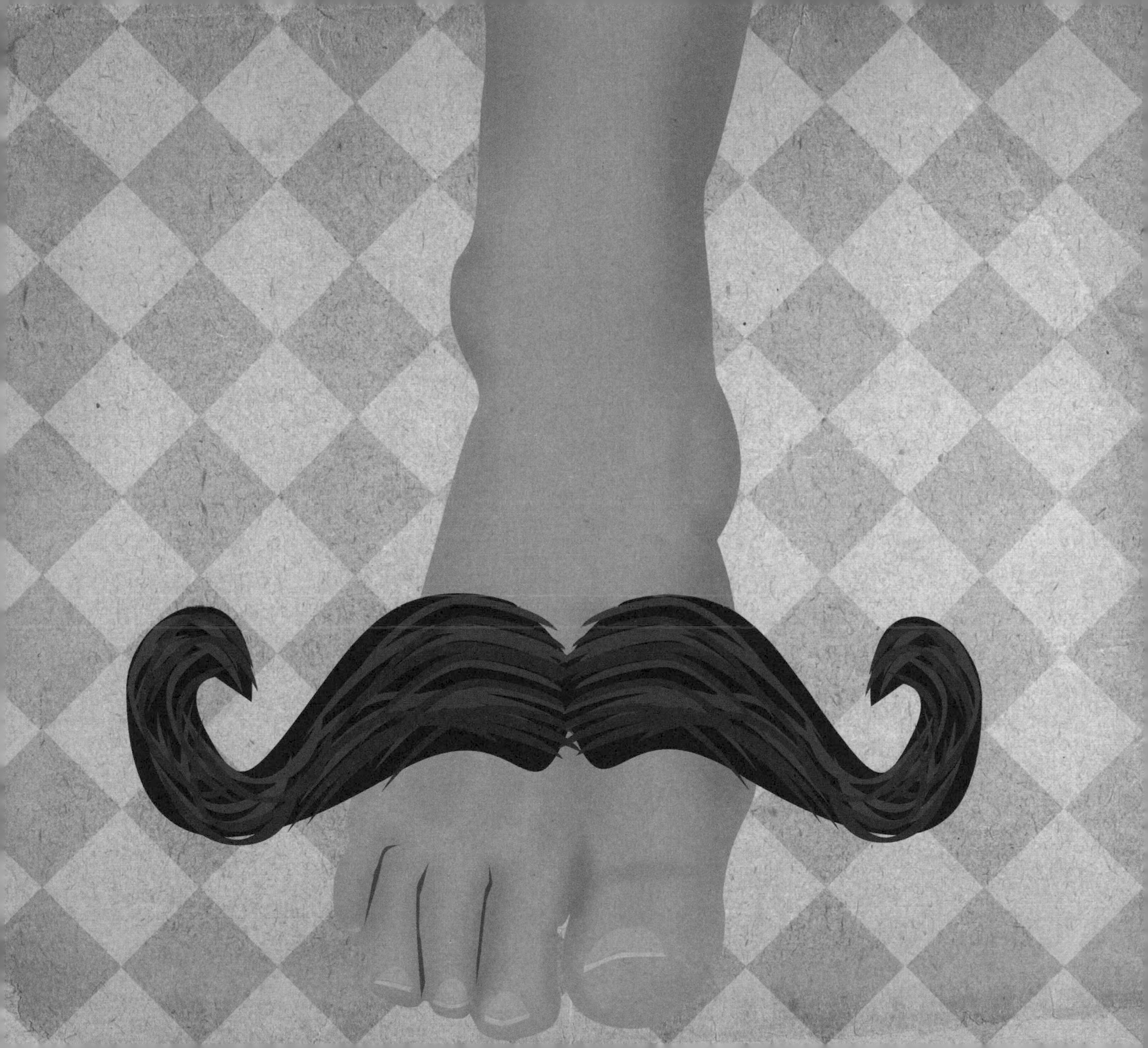

YUP,
THAT
SWORD
IS WET.

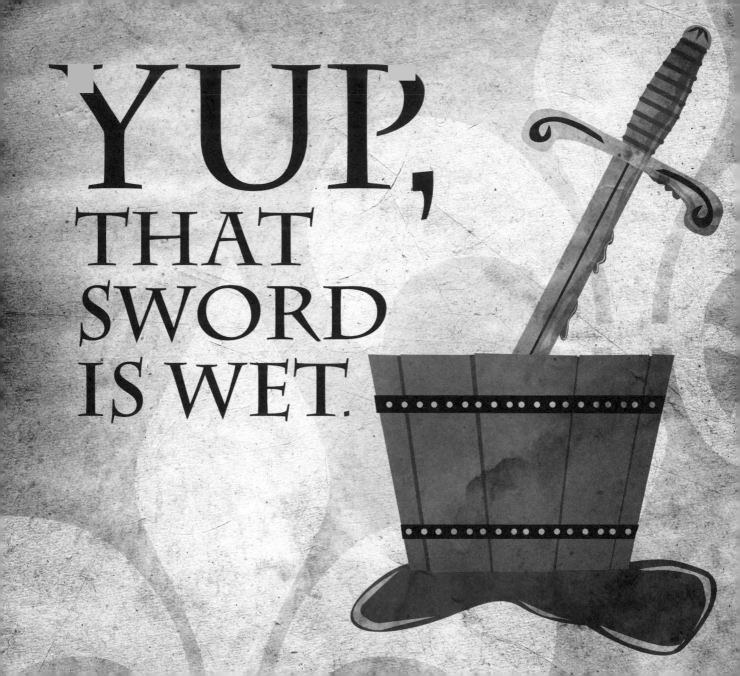

What are you doing?

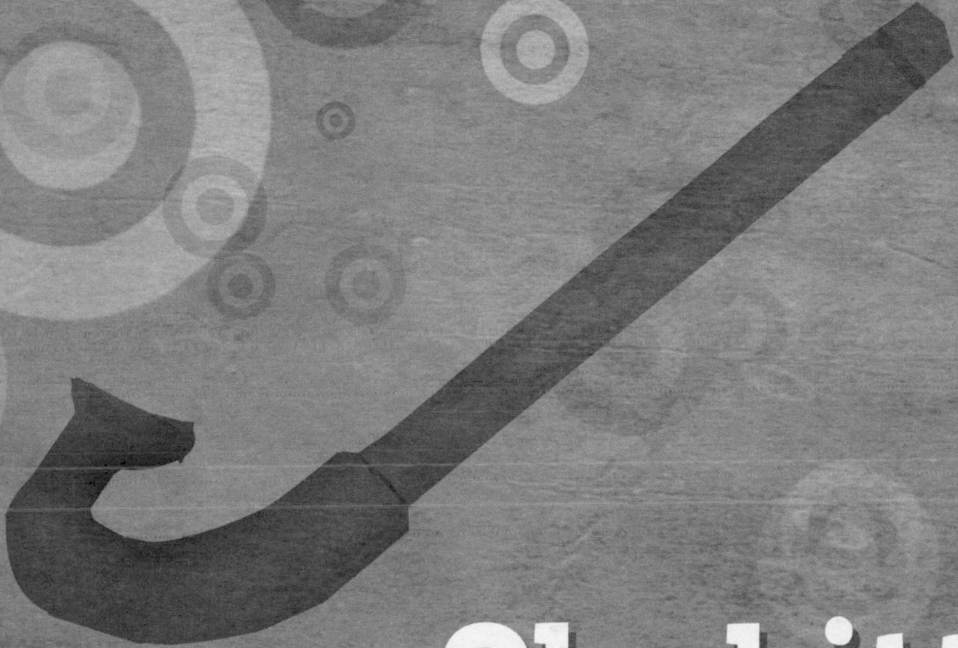

Oh, hitting the cat door with a snorkel.

Put the hatchet down, it's time to get jammies on.

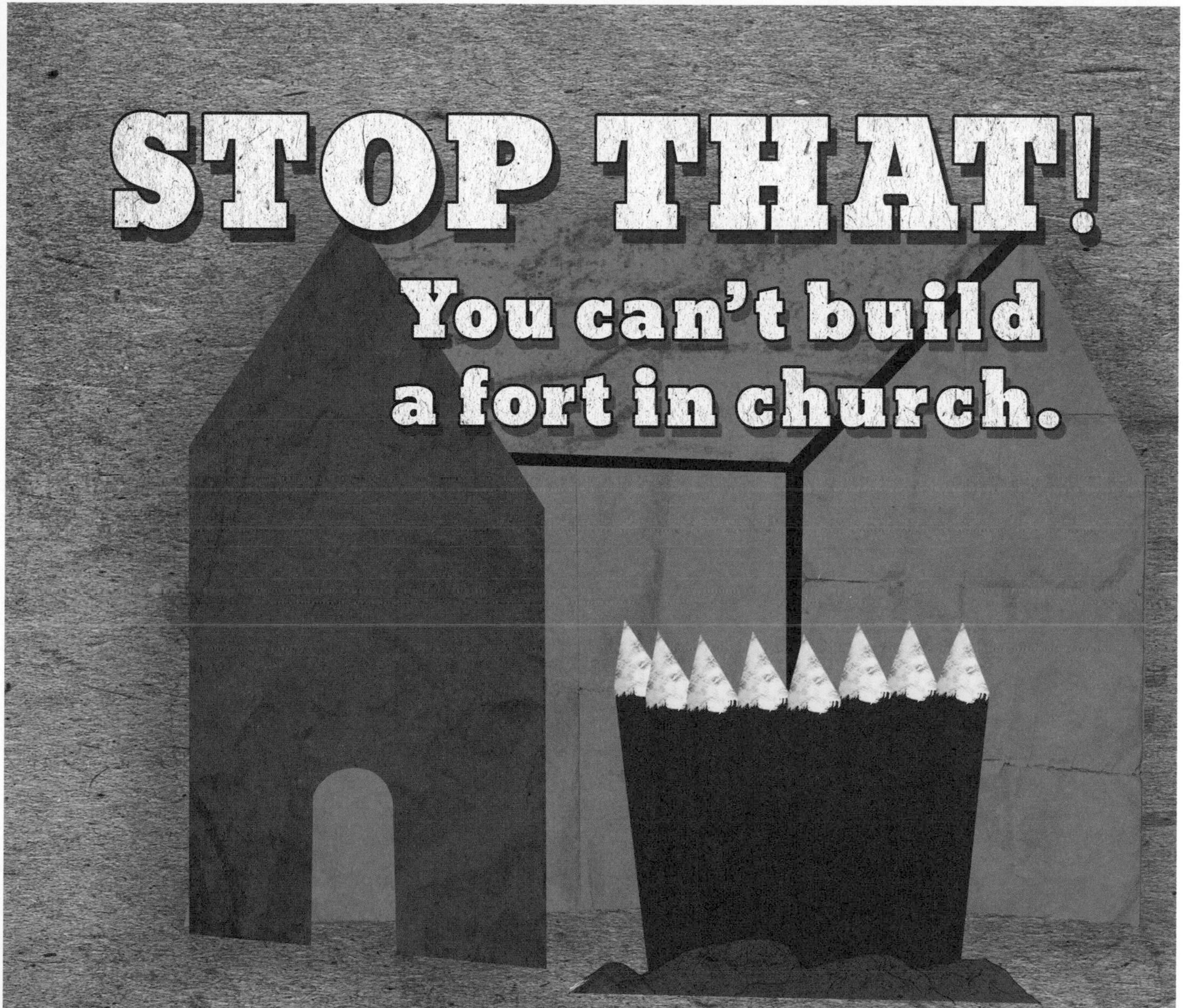
STOP THAT!
You can't build
a fort in church.

We don't clean the fridge with a banana.

Remove the ukulele from the ironing board.

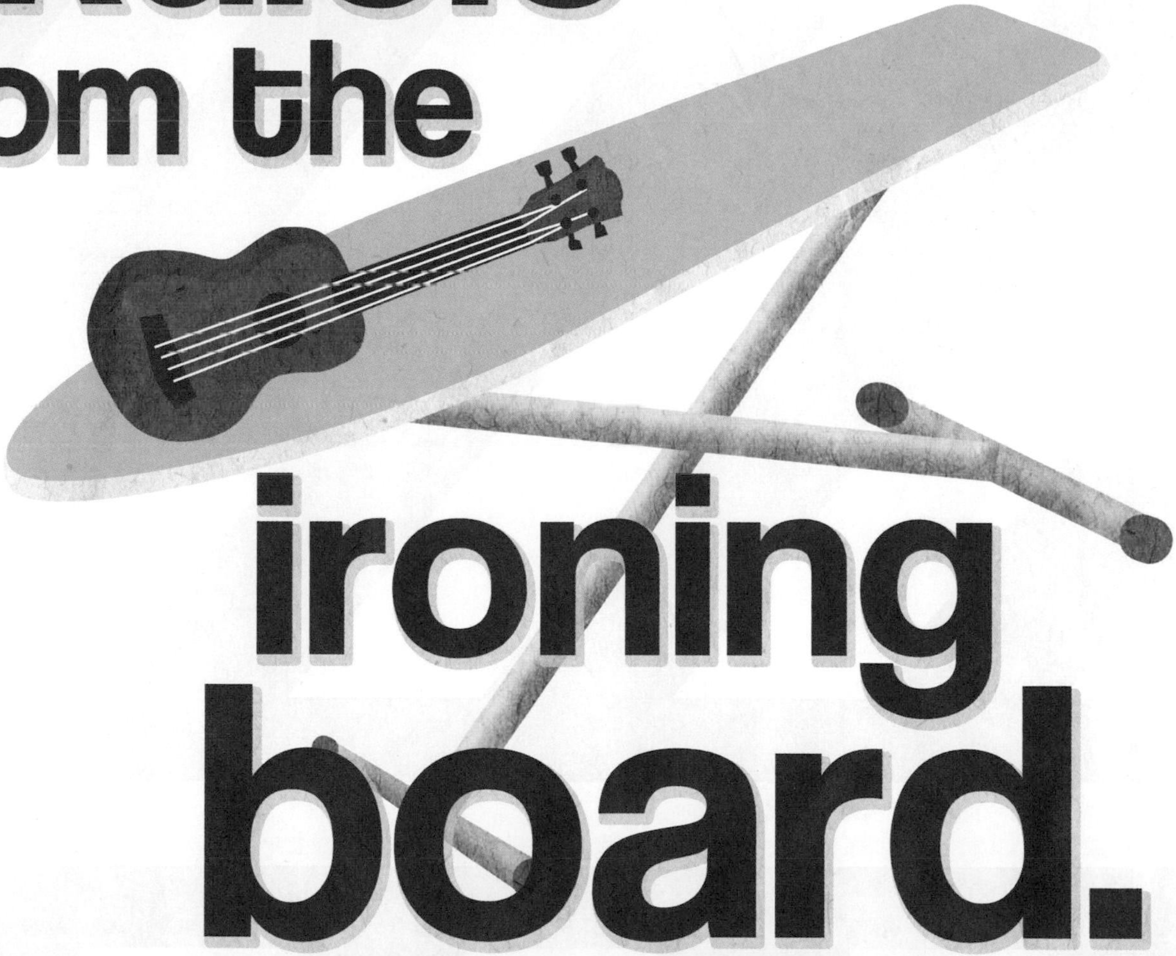

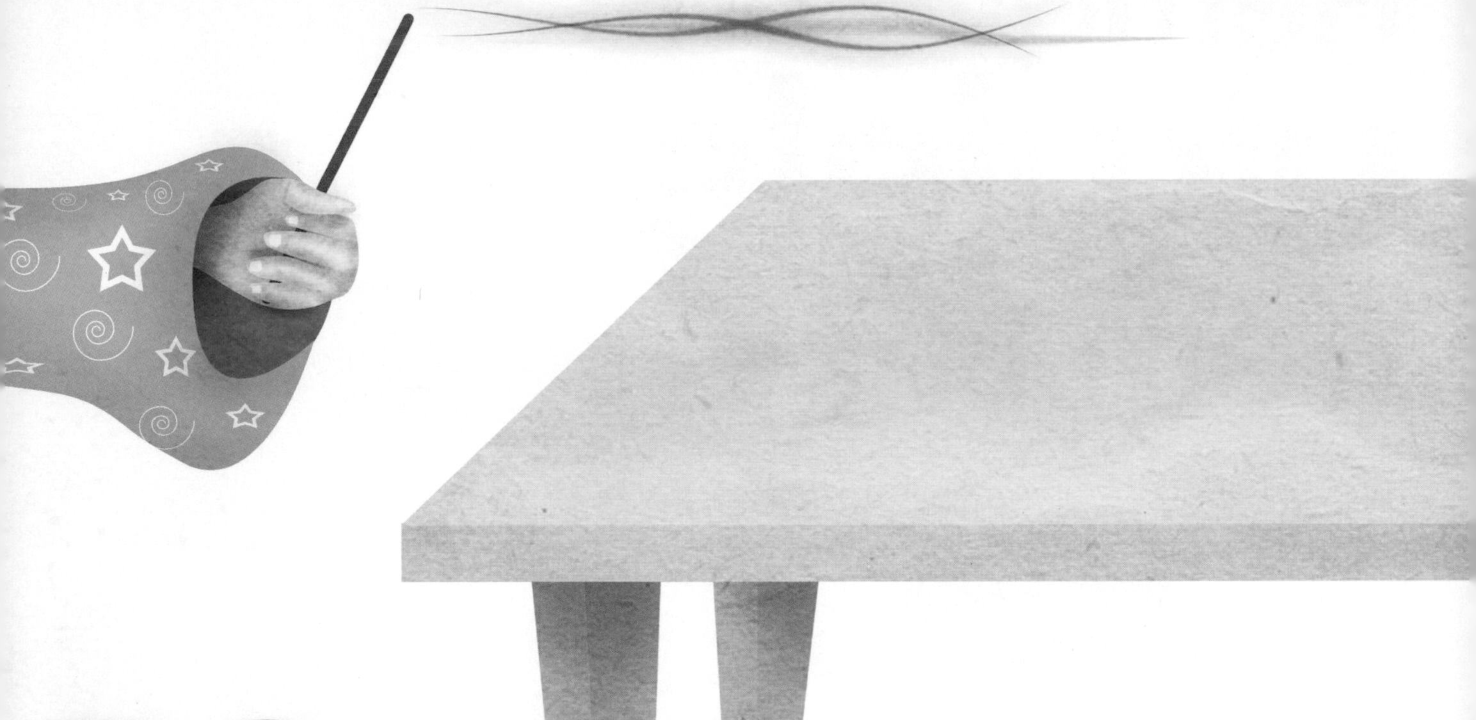

NO WANDS AT THE DINNER TABLE.

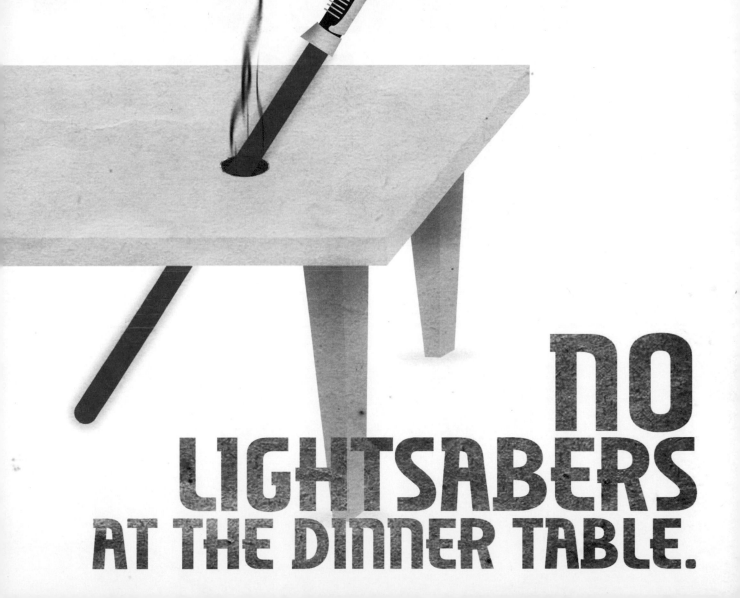

NO
LIGHTSABERS
AT THE DINNER TABLE.

T. REXES DO NOT EAT CRACKERS.

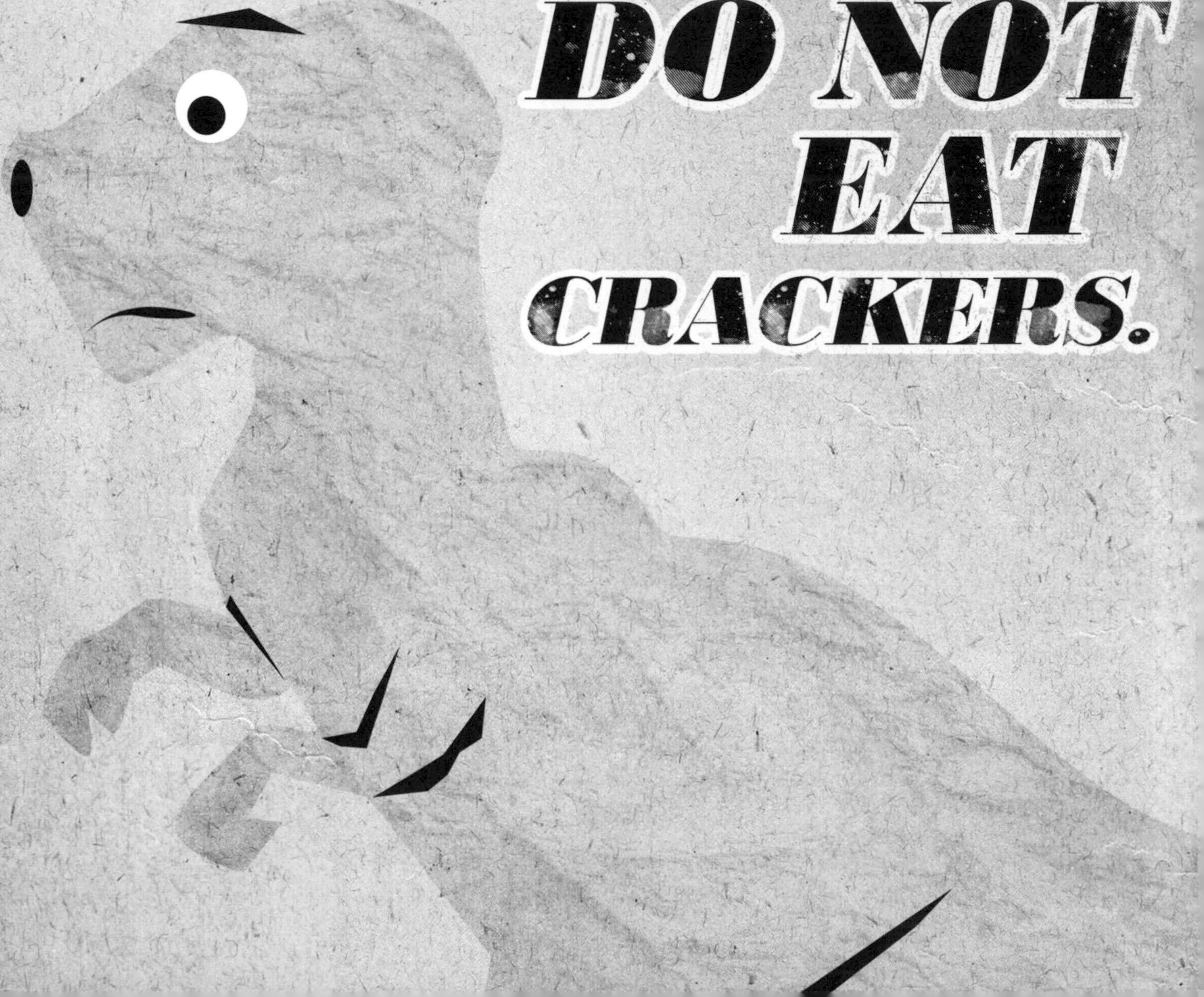

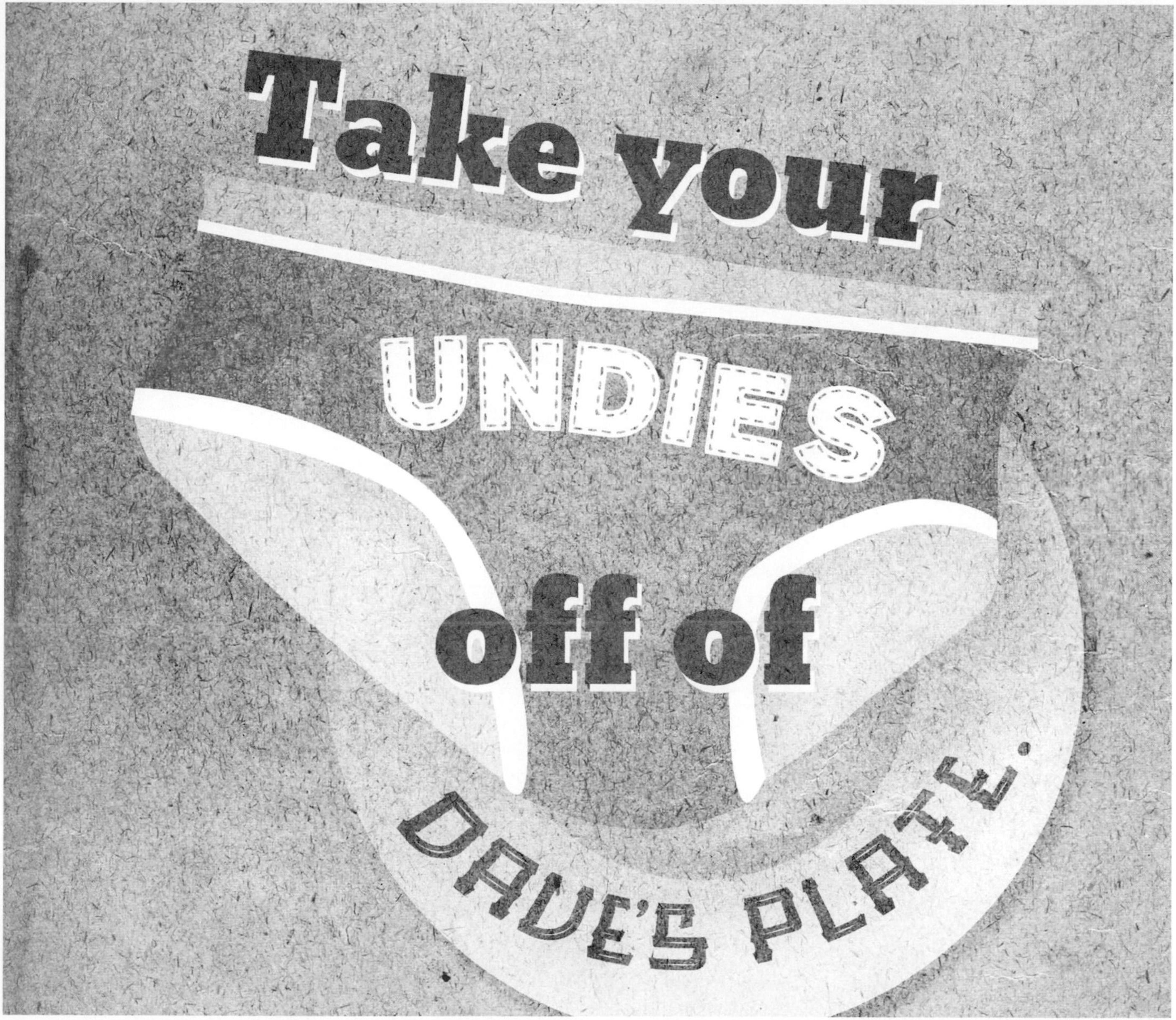
Take your
UNDIES
off of
DAVE'S PLATE.

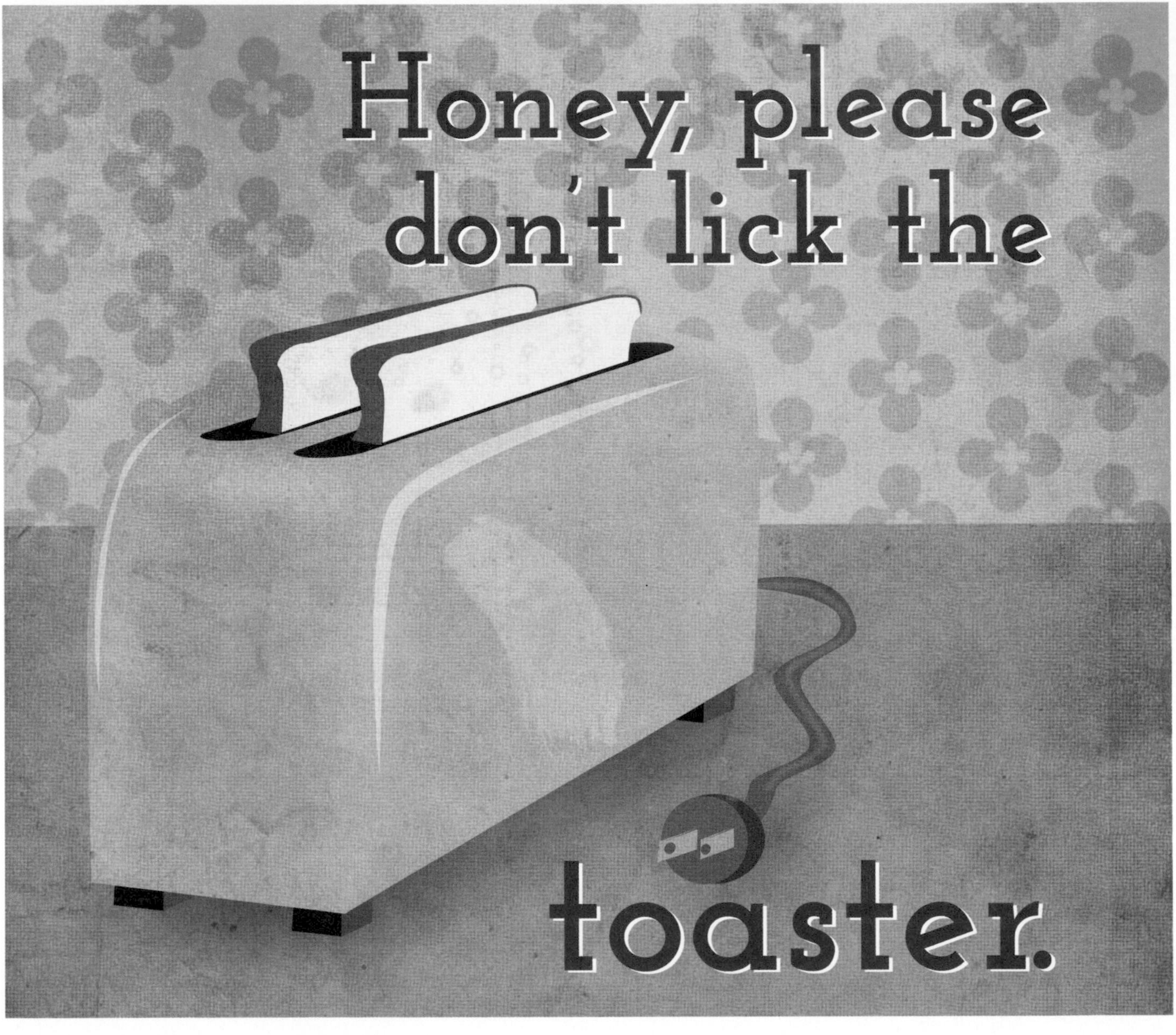
Honey, please don't lick the
toaster.

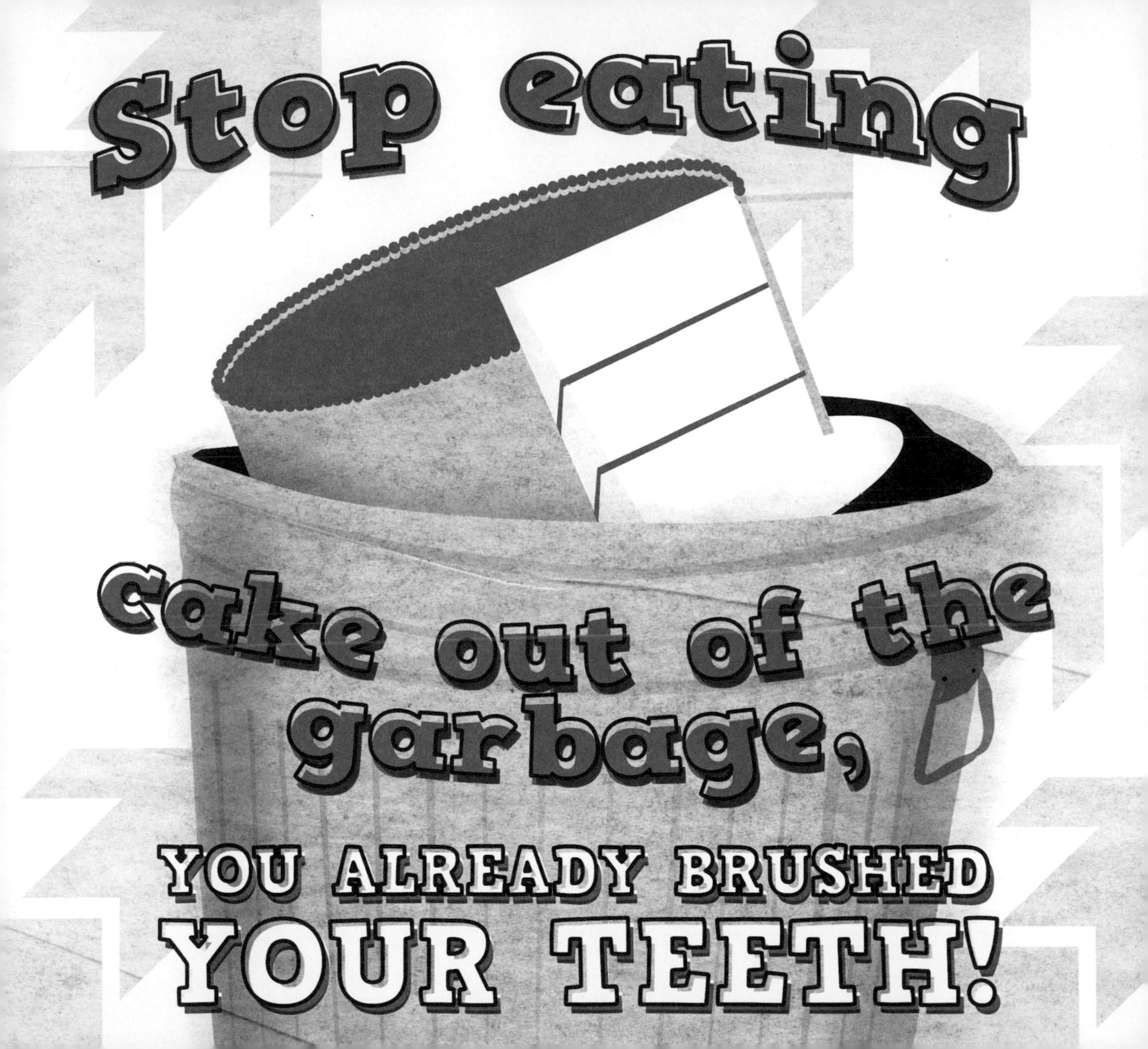
Stop eating
cake out of the
garbage,
YOU ALREADY BRUSHED
YOUR TEETH!

Stop licking your *ARMPITS* and play some dodgeball.

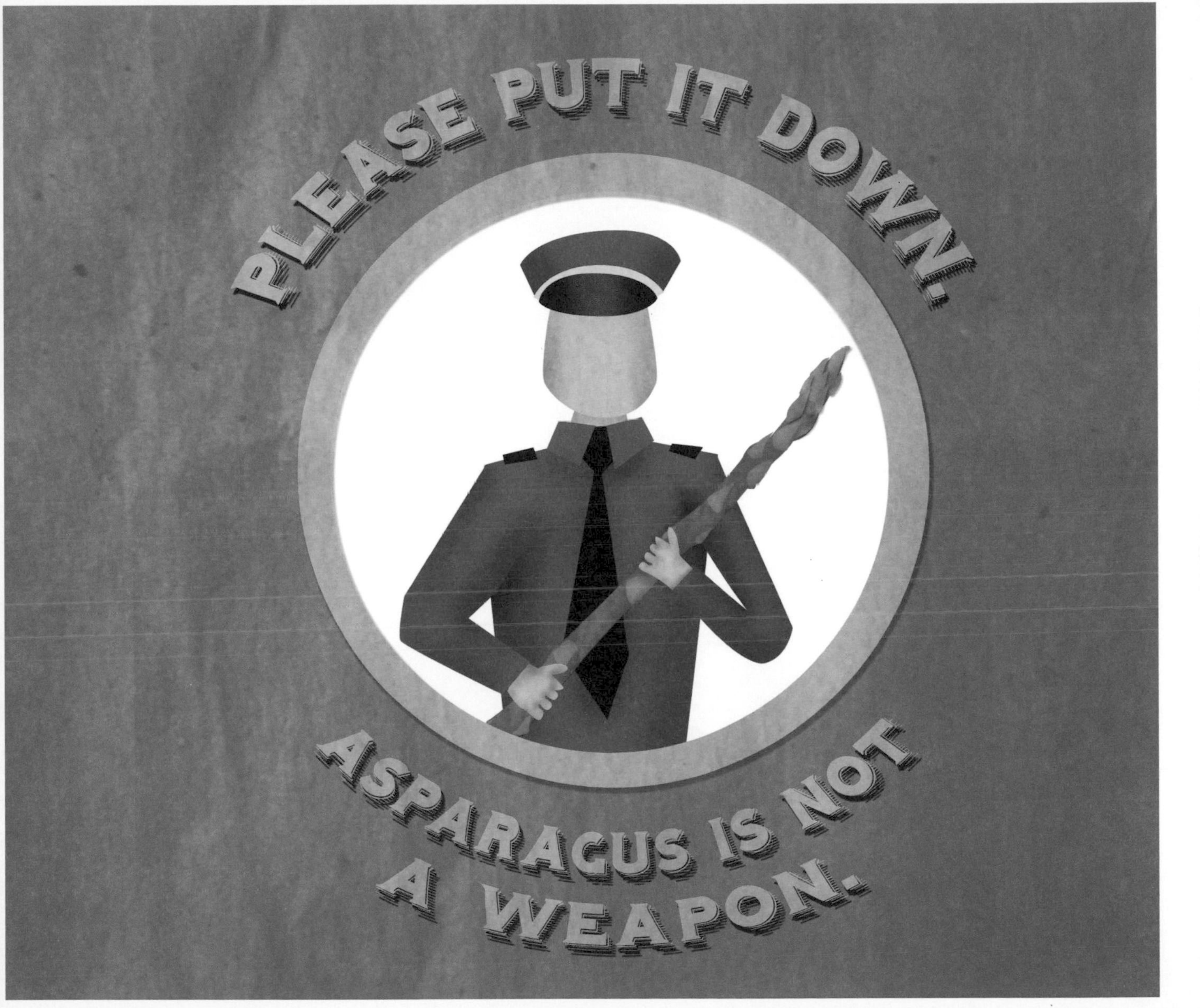
PLEASE PUT IT DOWN.
ASPARAGUS IS NOT A WEAPON.

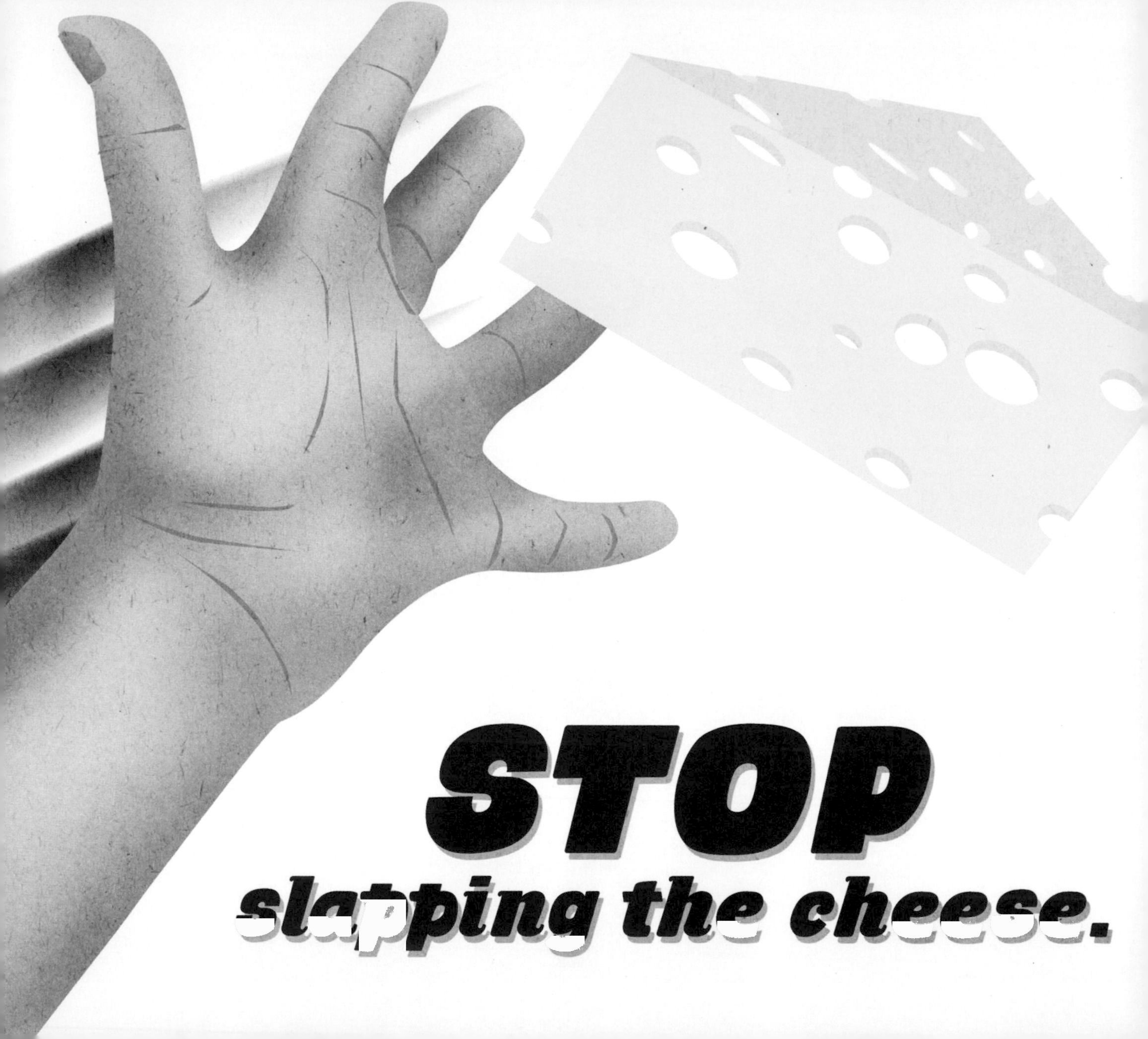
STOP
slapping the cheese.

STOP
rubbing watermelon on your arm.

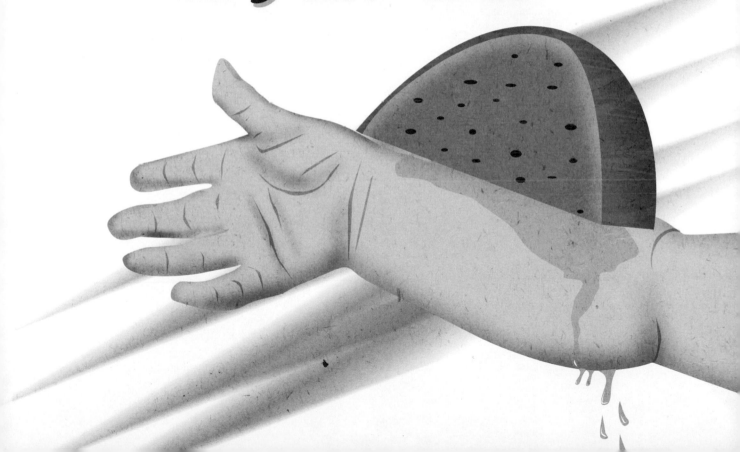

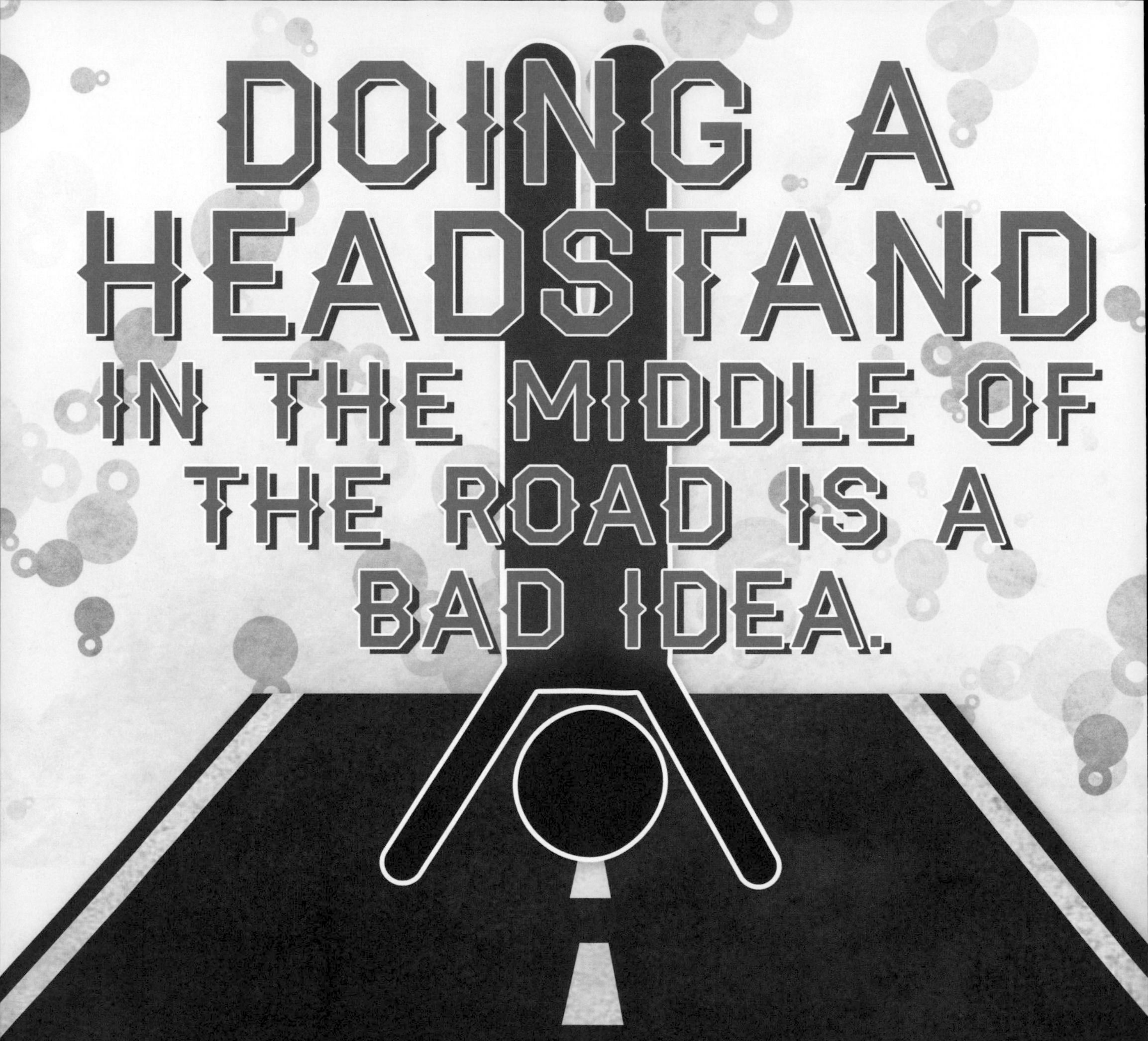
DOING A HEADSTAND IN THE MIDDLE OF THE ROAD IS A BAD IDEA.

WE DO NOT POOP IN BOOKS.

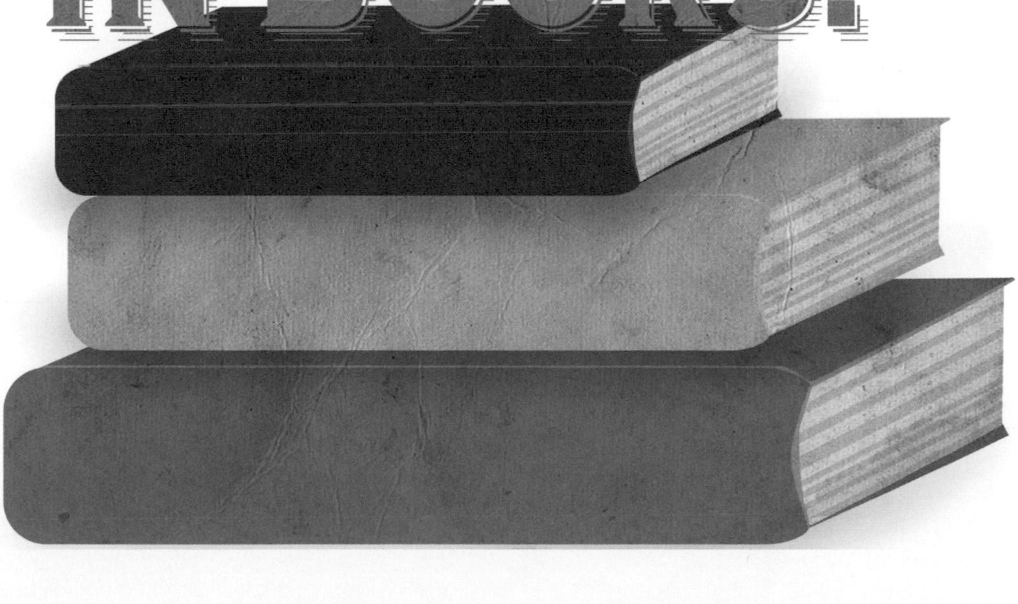

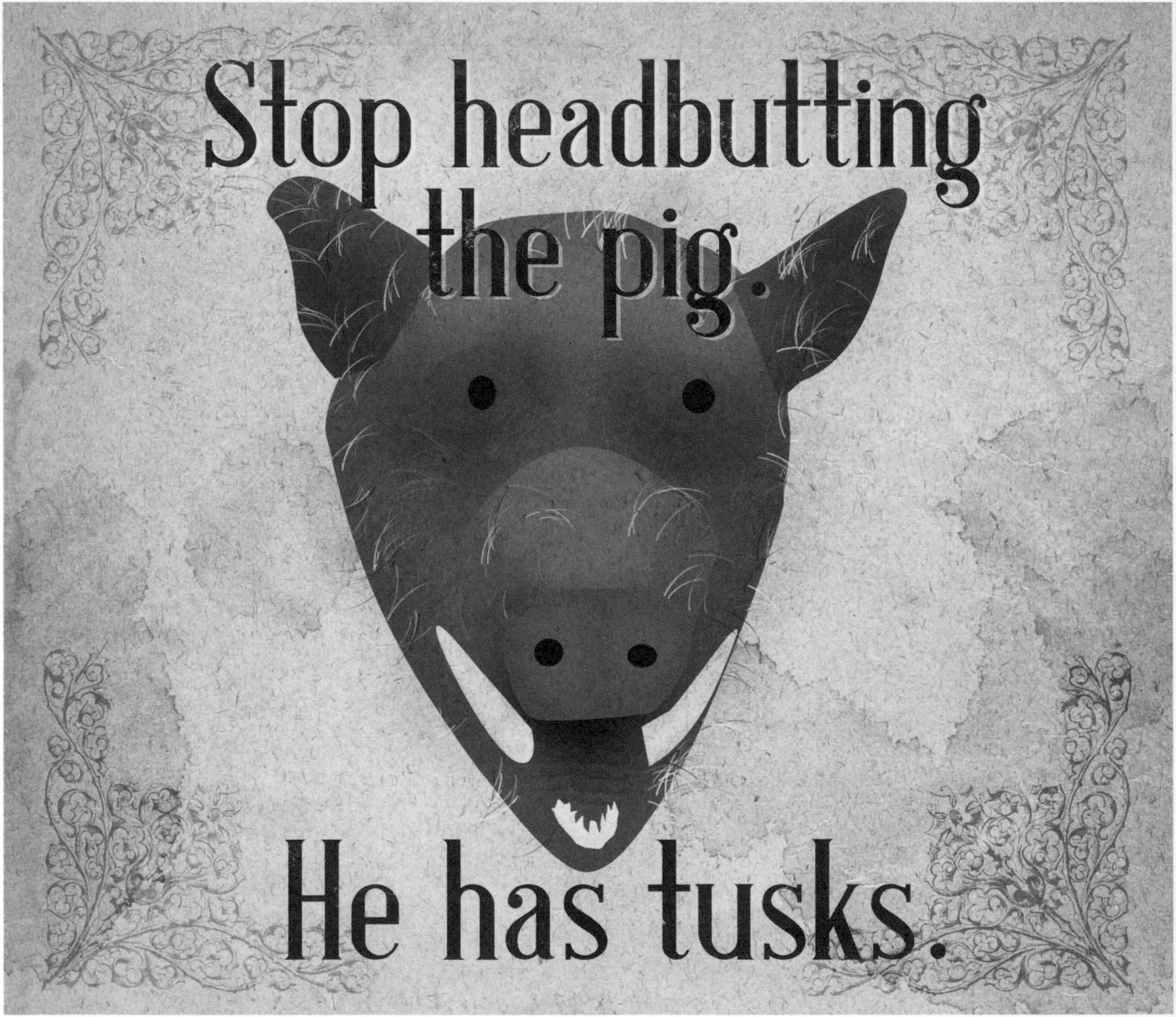
Stop headbutting the pig.
He has tusks.

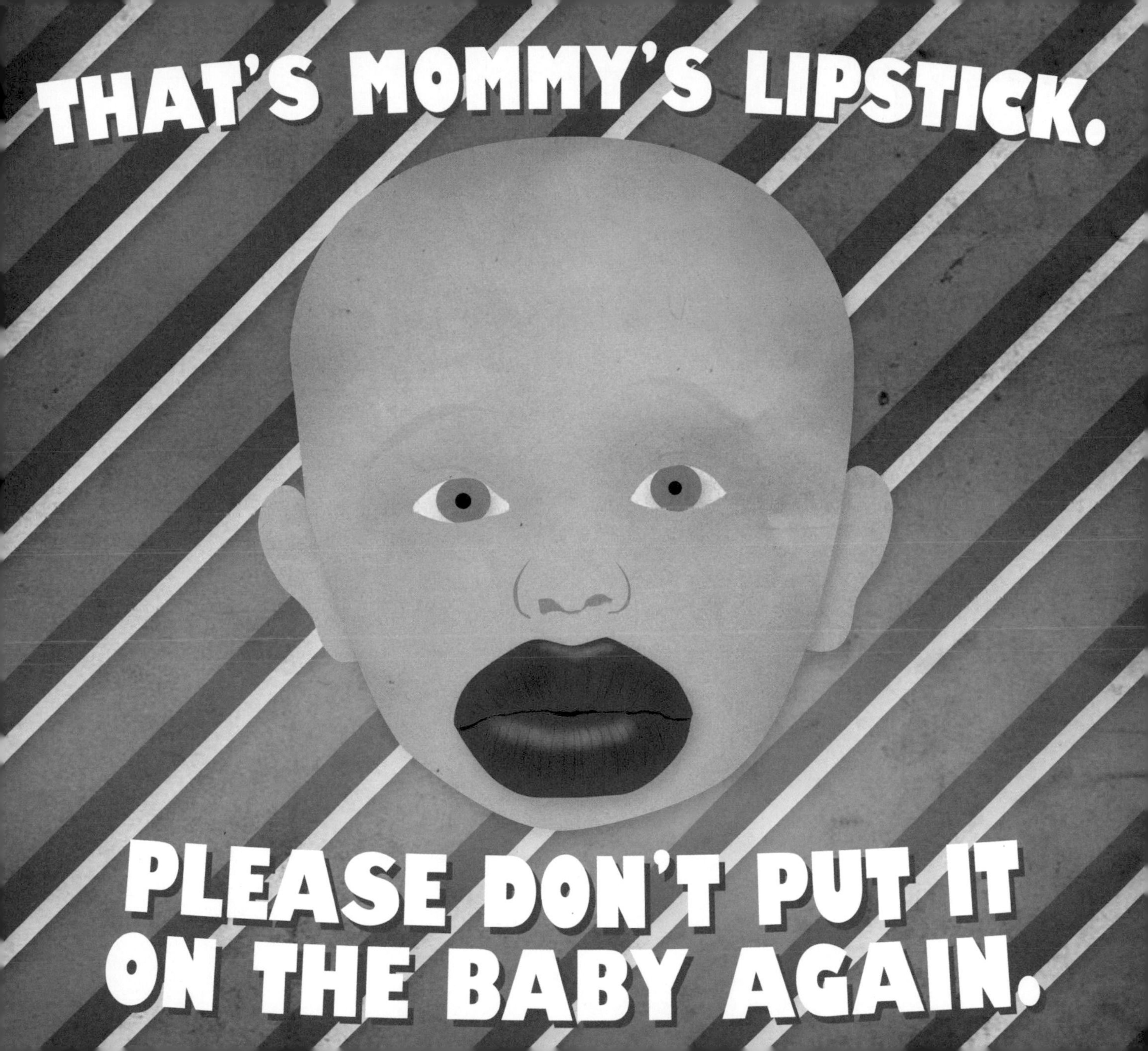
THAT'S MOMMY'S LIPSTICK.
PLEASE DON'T PUT IT ON THE BABY AGAIN.

Stop putting popcorn kernels up the dog's nose!

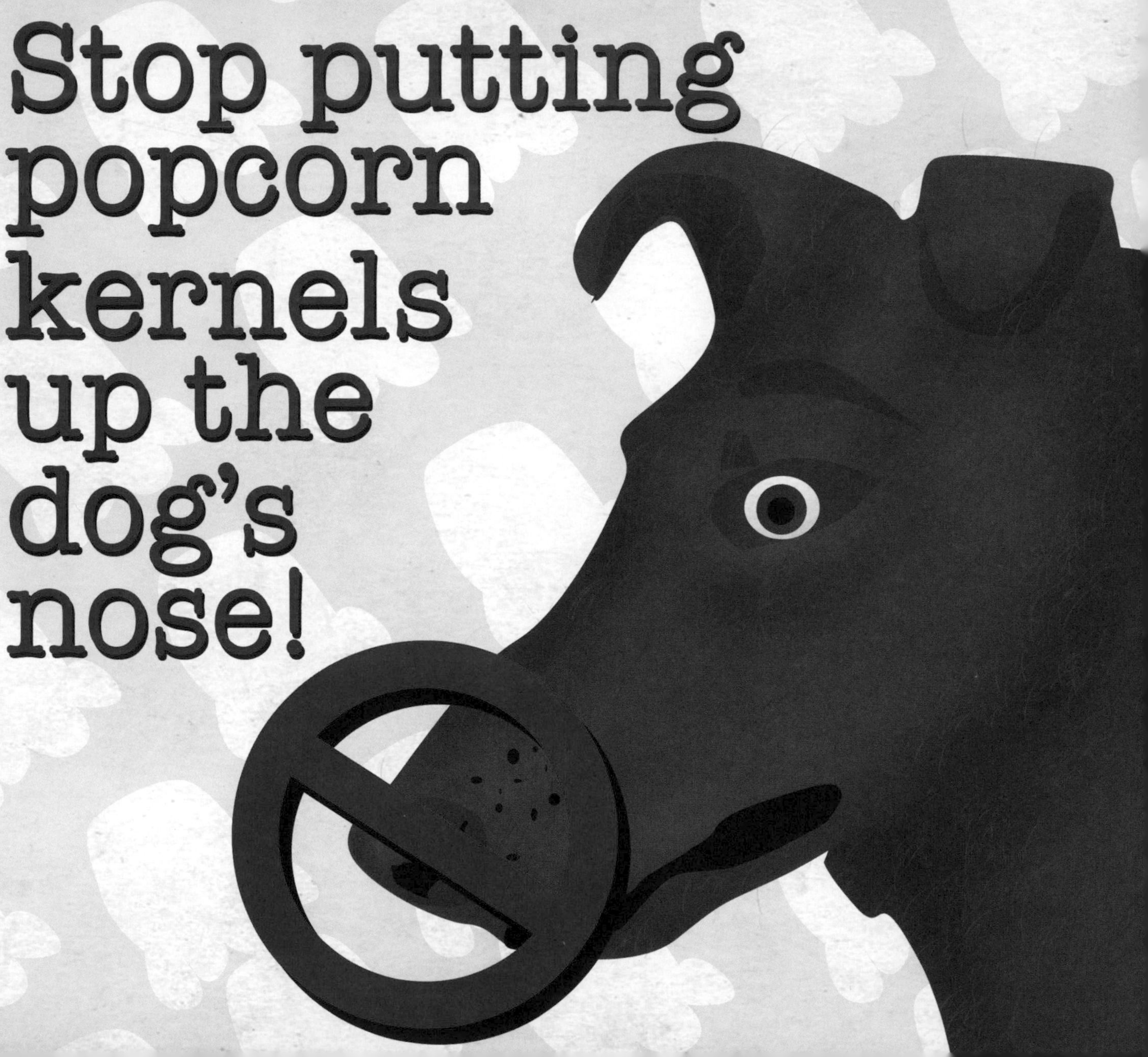

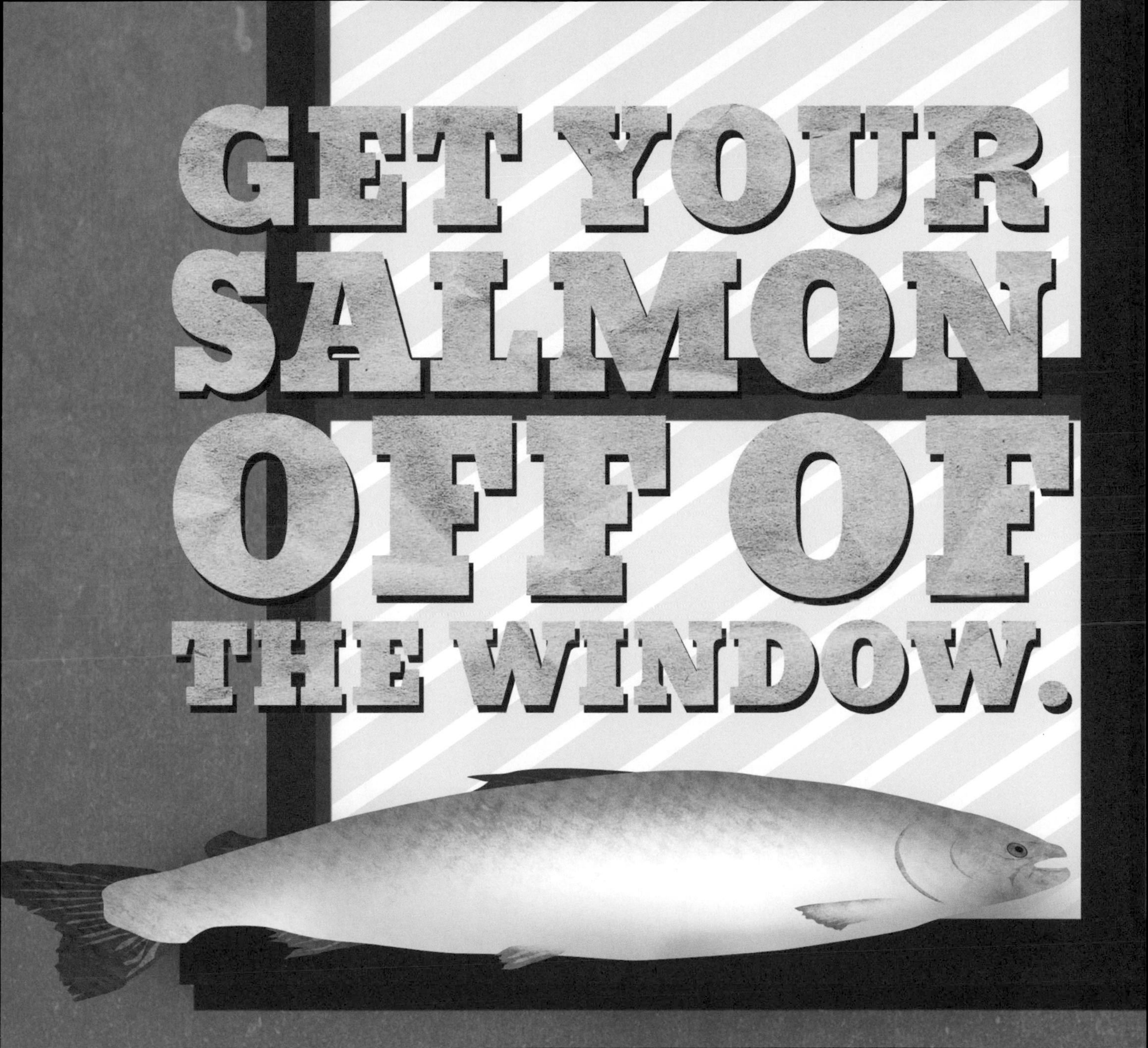
GET YOUR
SALMON
OFF OF
THE WINDOW.

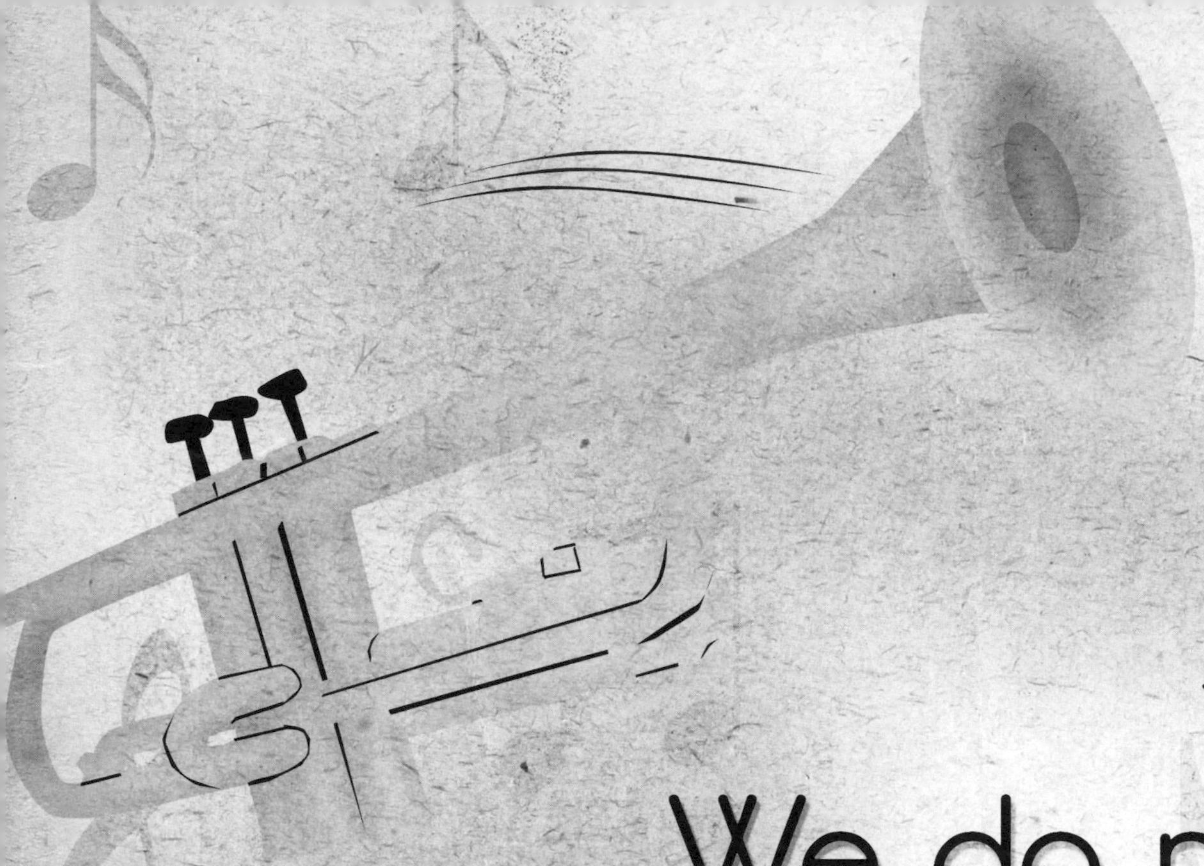

We do not hit our friends with musical instruments.

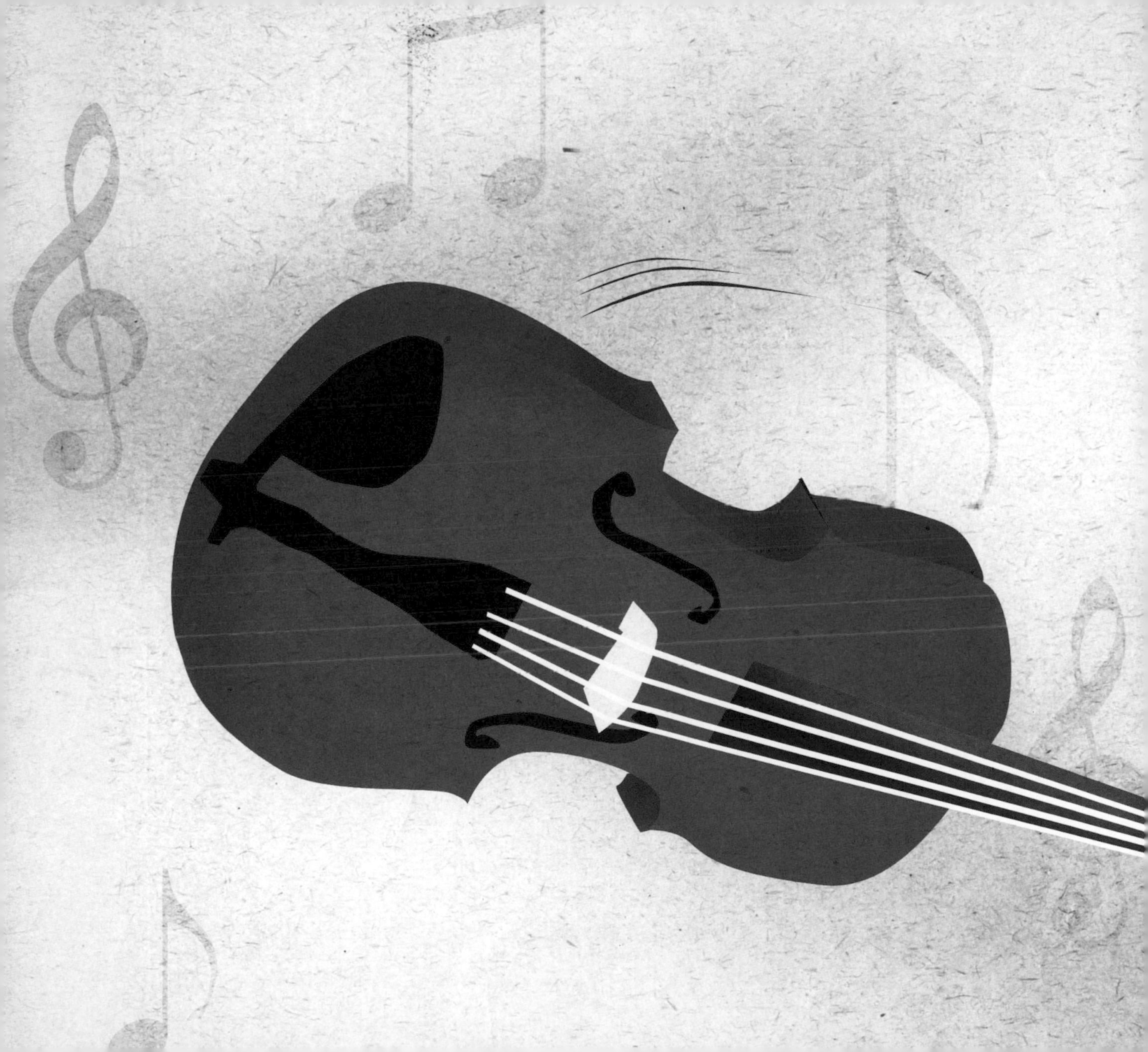

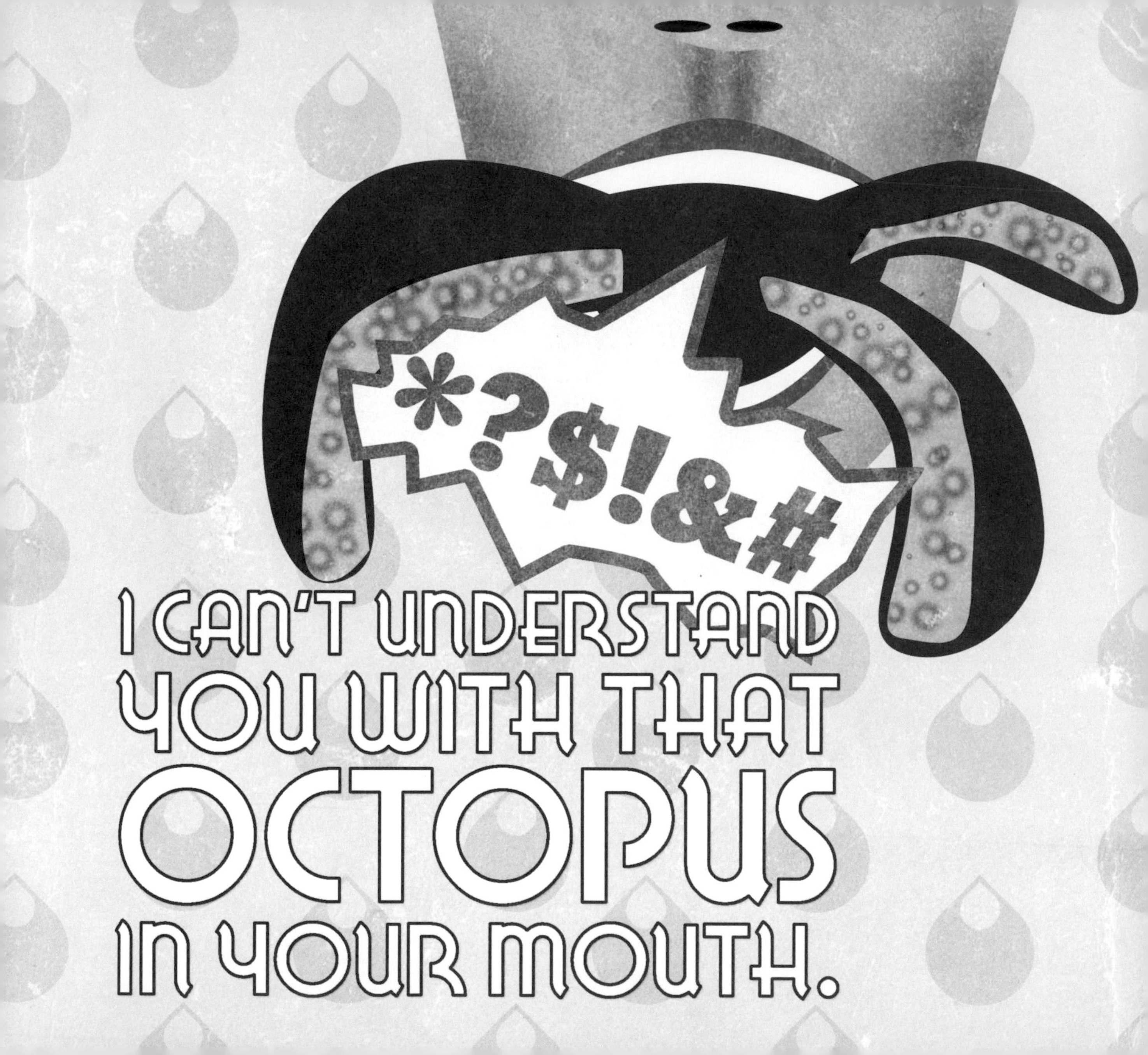
*?$!&#
I CAN'T UNDERSTAND YOU WITH THAT OCTOPUS IN YOUR MOUTH.

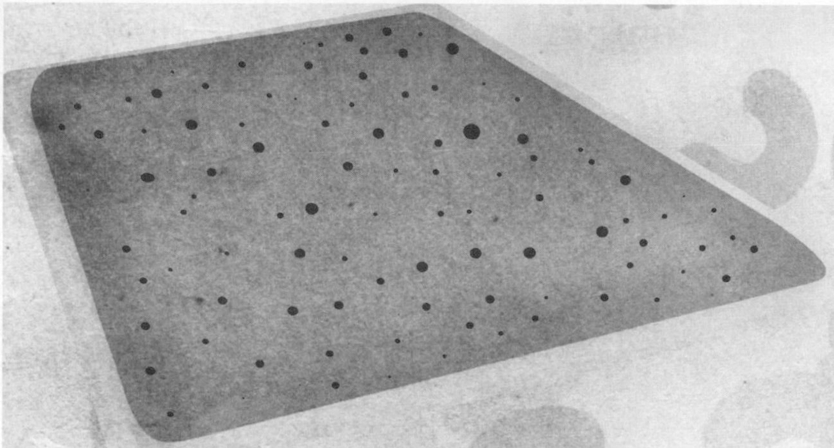

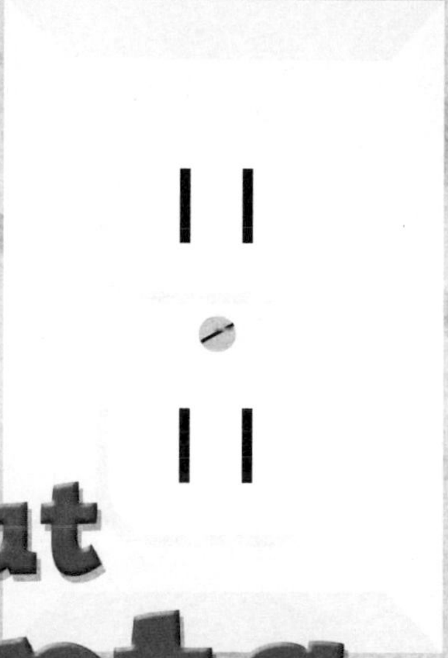

NO!

We don't put

Pop-Tarts

in the

electrical outlets.

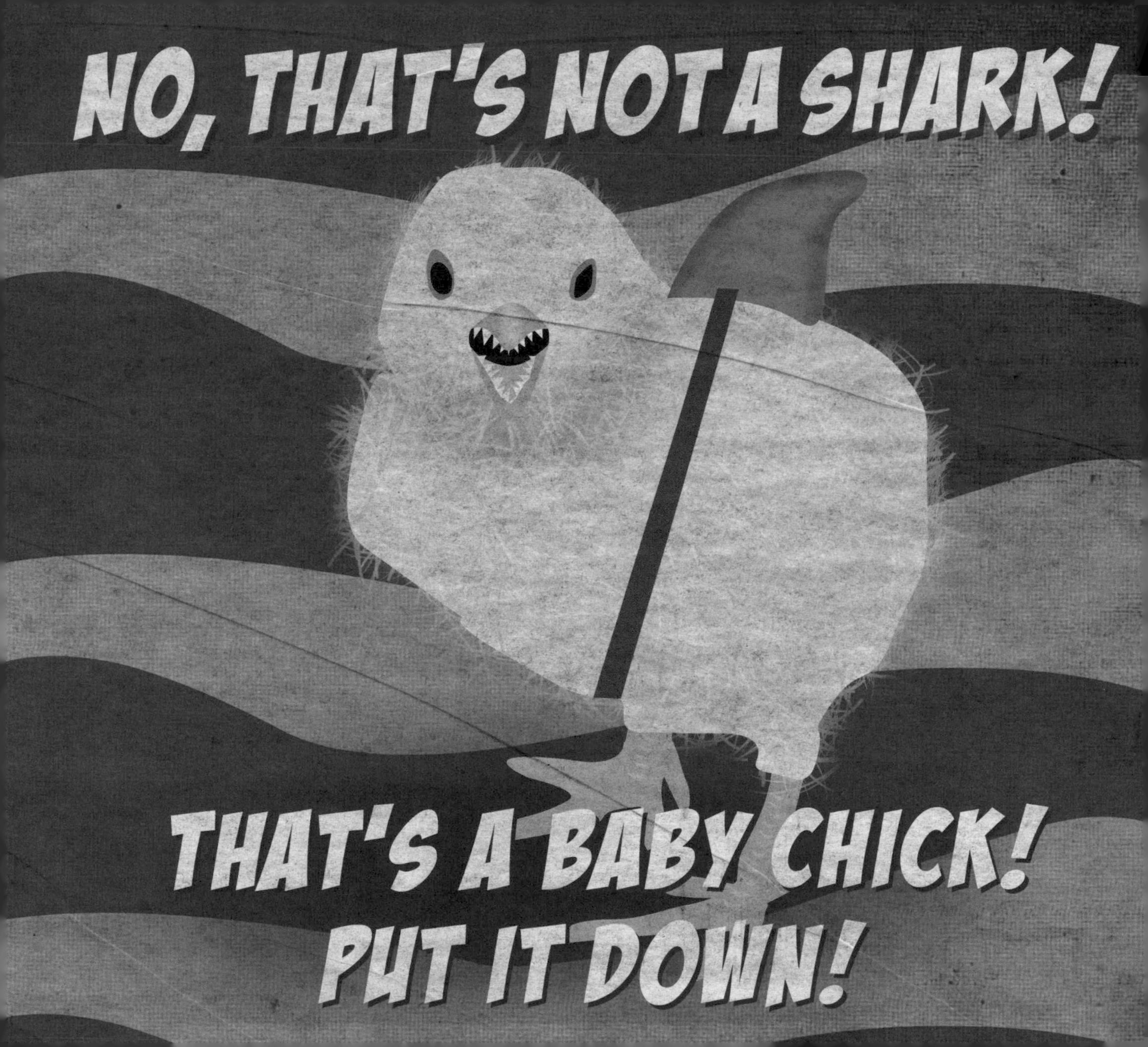
NO, THAT'S NOT A SHARK!
THAT'S A BABY CHICK!
PUT IT DOWN!

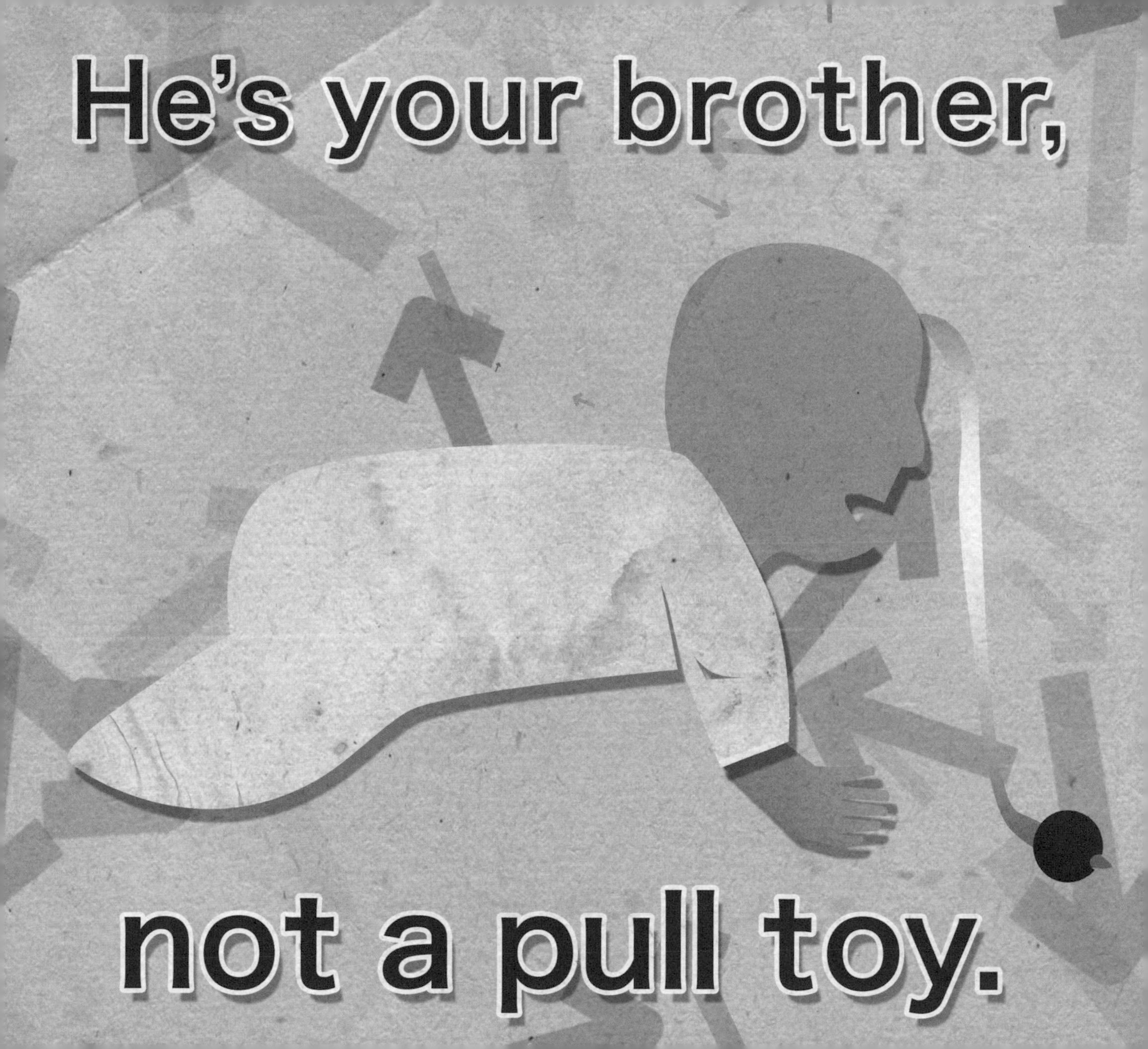
He's your brother,
not a pull toy.

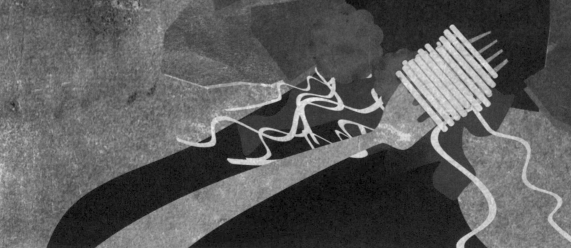

QUIT PUTTING SPAGHETTI IN THE BAT CAVE.

Get off the cat, he is not a pony.

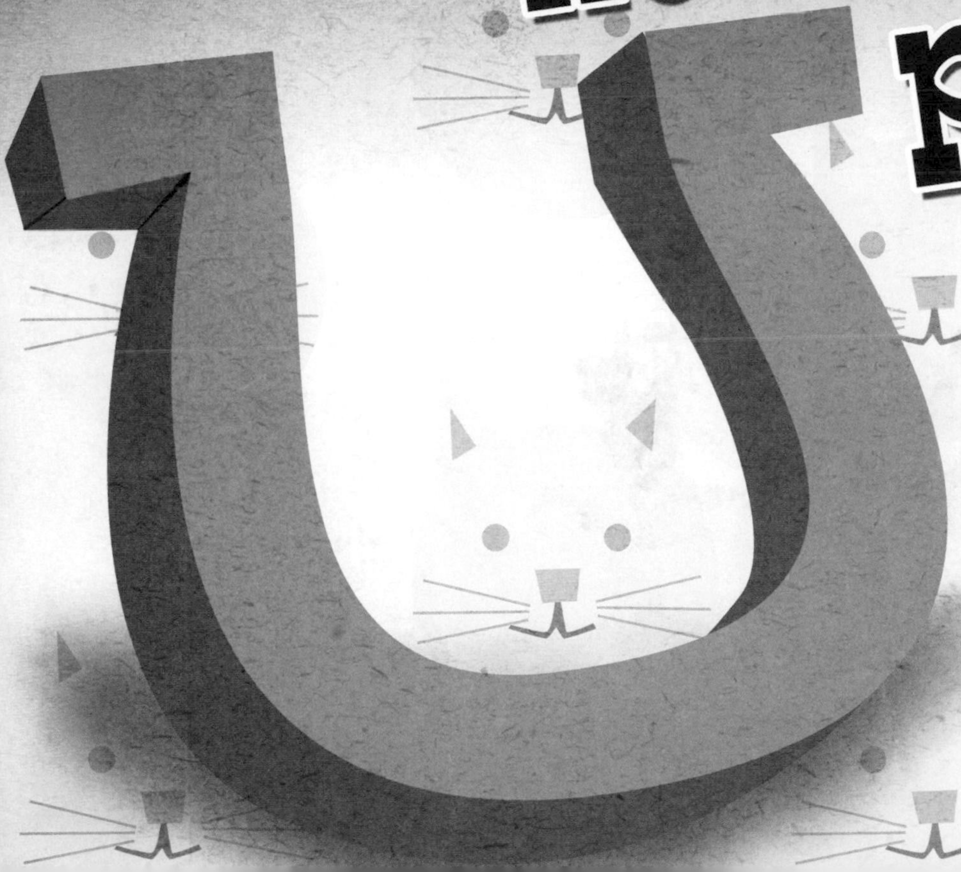

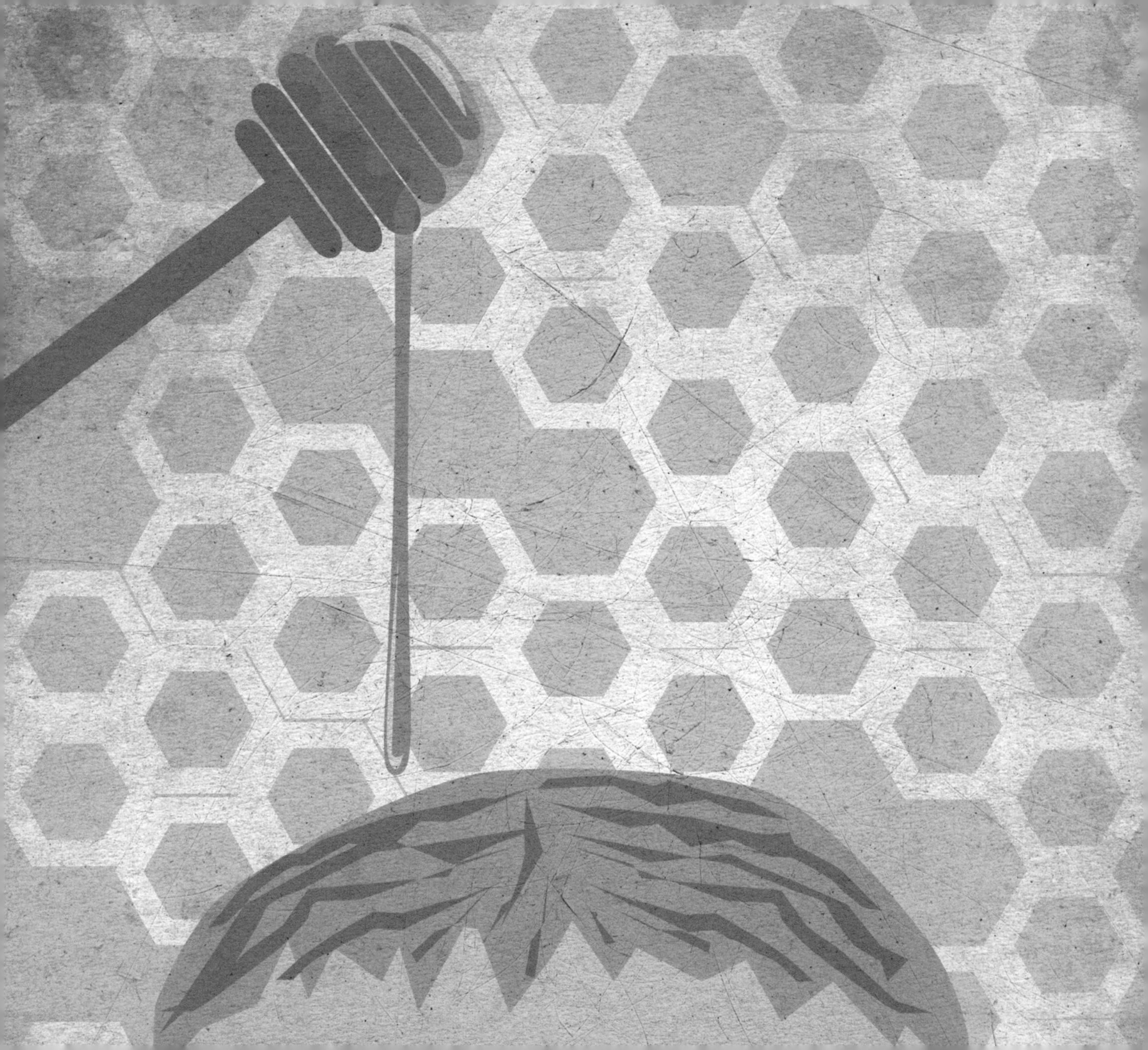

Did you put honey on your brother's head?

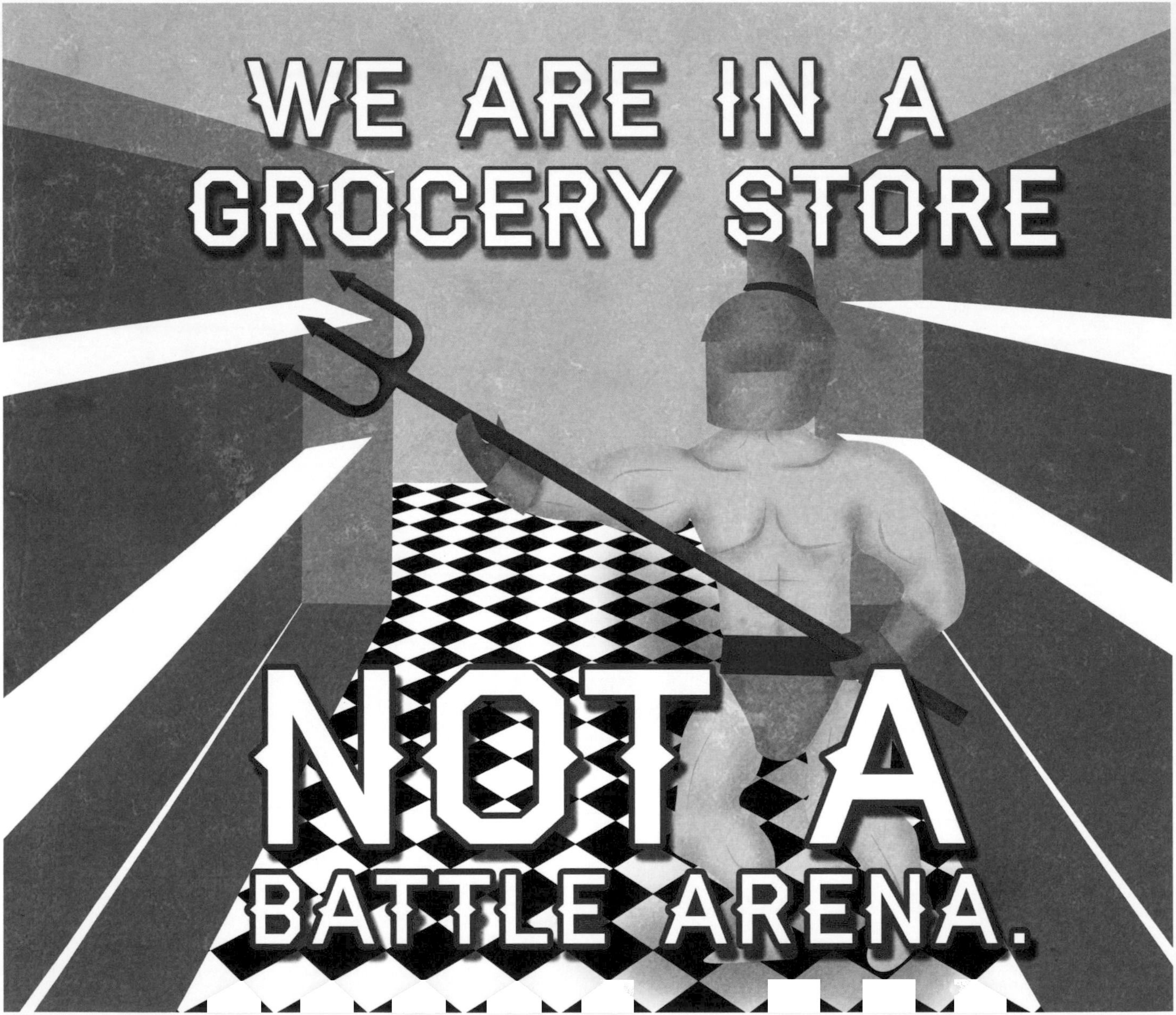
WE ARE IN A
GROCERY STORE
NOT A
BATTLE ARENA.

THIS IS WHY
I TOLD YOU

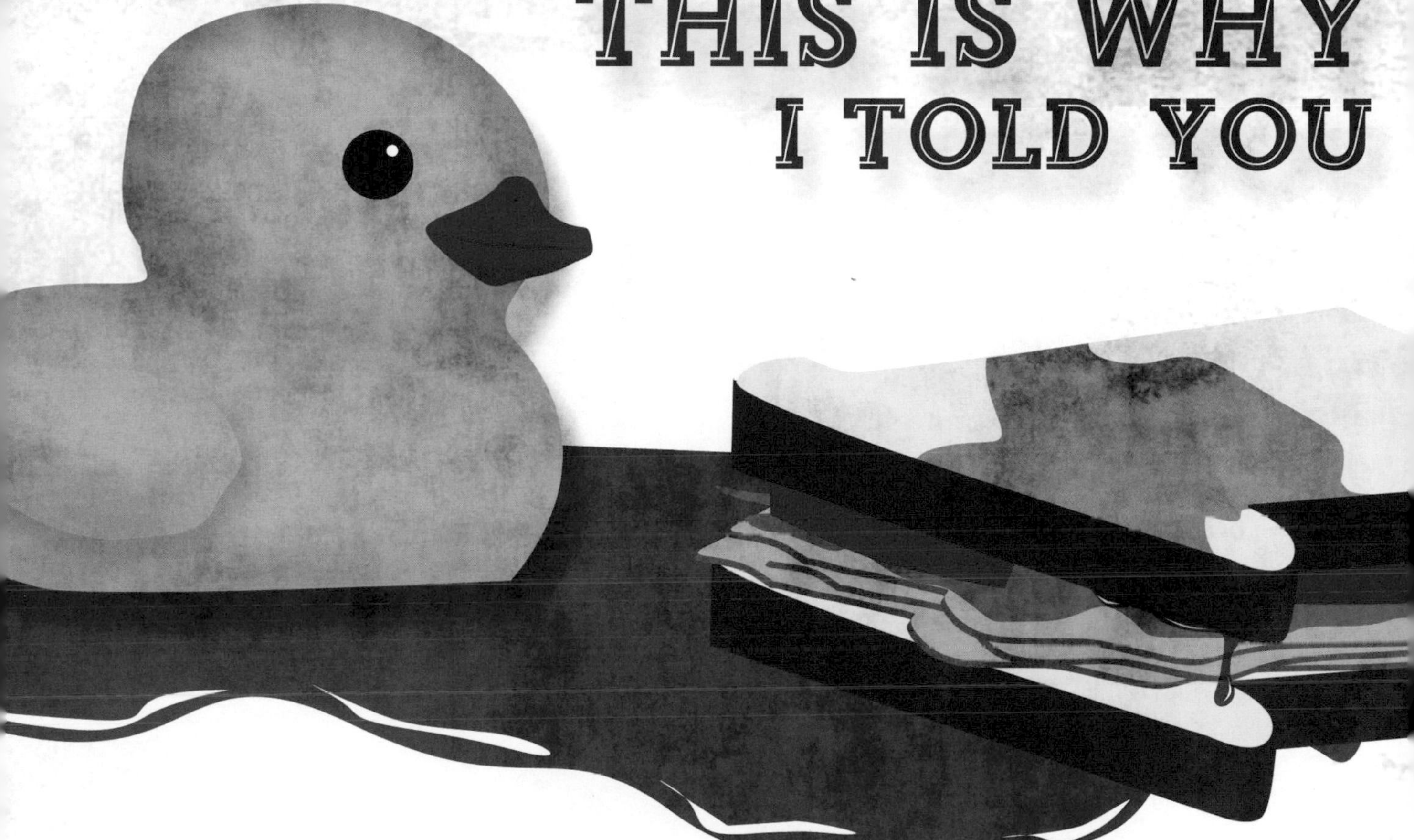

YOU COULD NOT
TAKE YOUR SANDWICH
INTO THE BATHTUB.

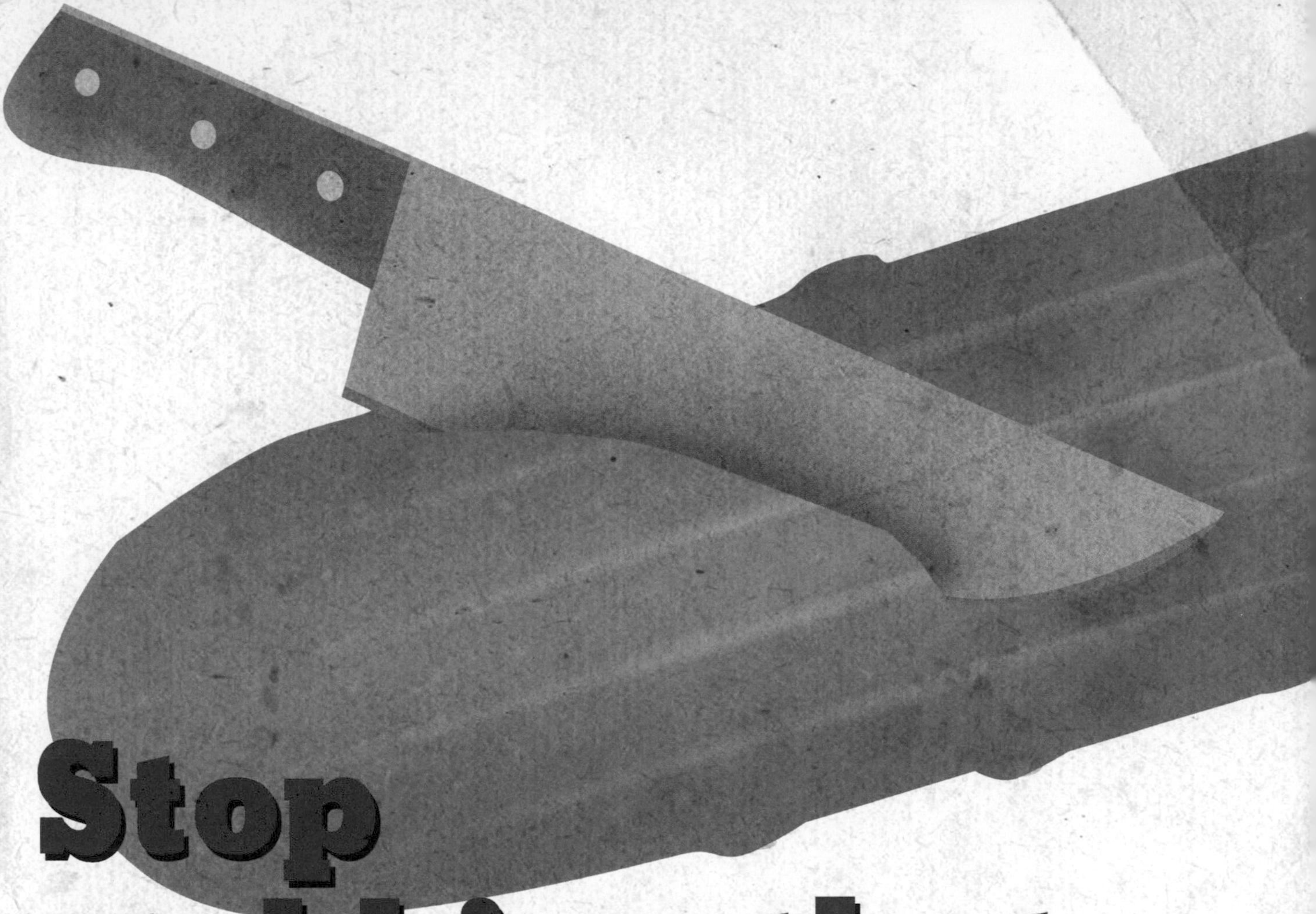

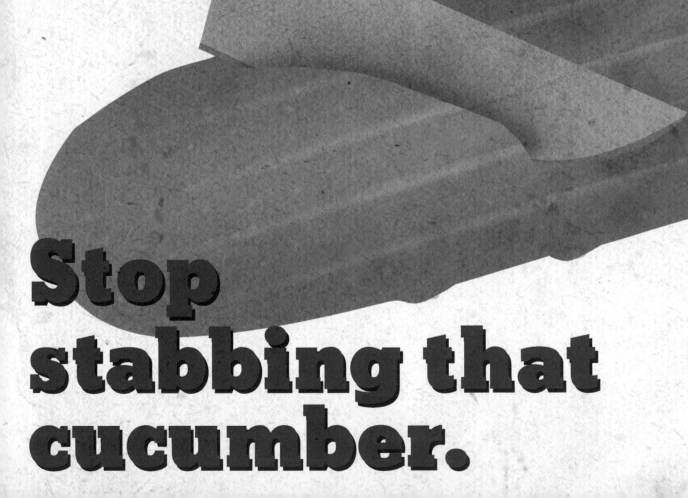

Stop stabbing that cucumber.

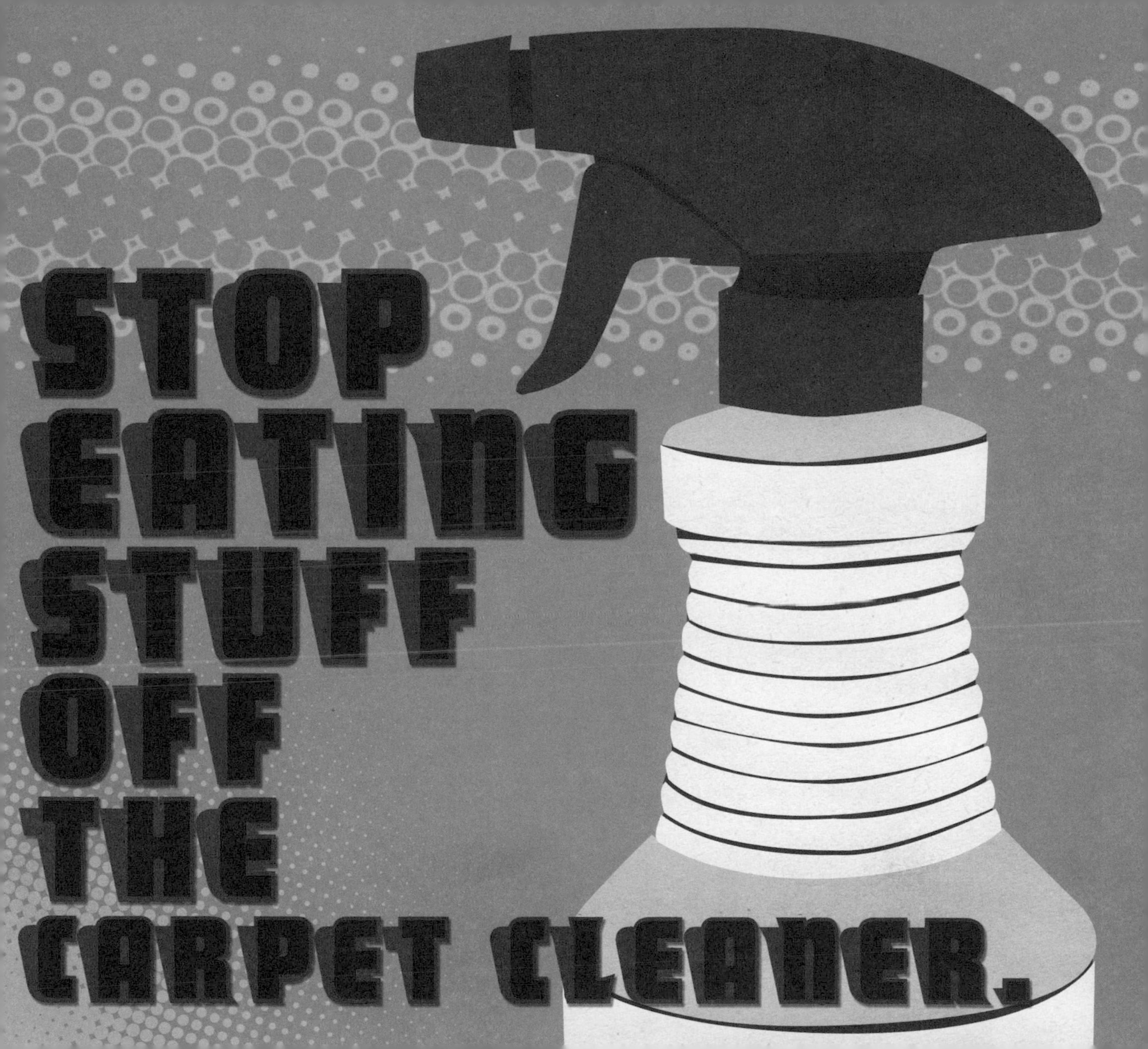
STOP EATING STUFF OFF THE CARPET CLEANER.

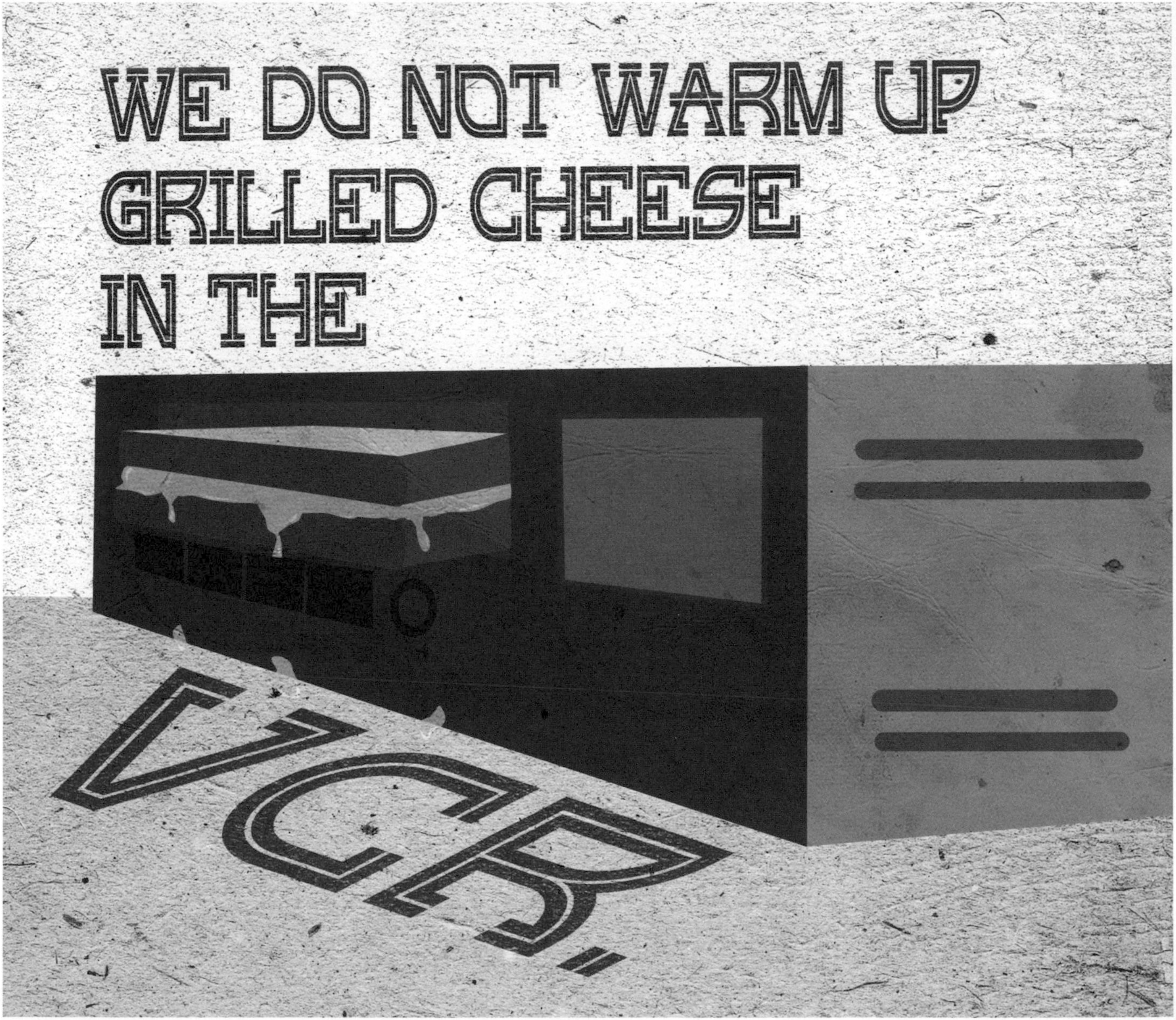
WE DO NOT WARM UP
GRILLED CHEESE
IN THE
VCR.

Why is there peanut butter in your ear?

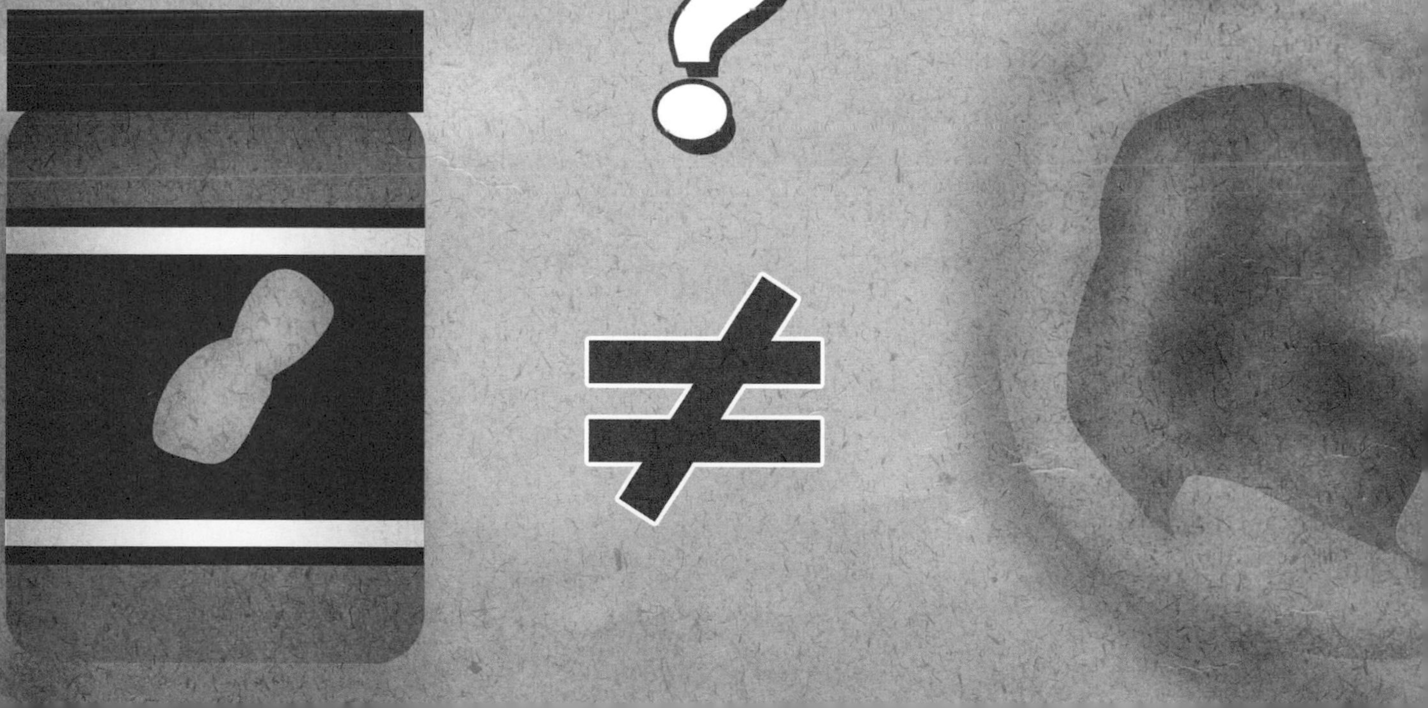

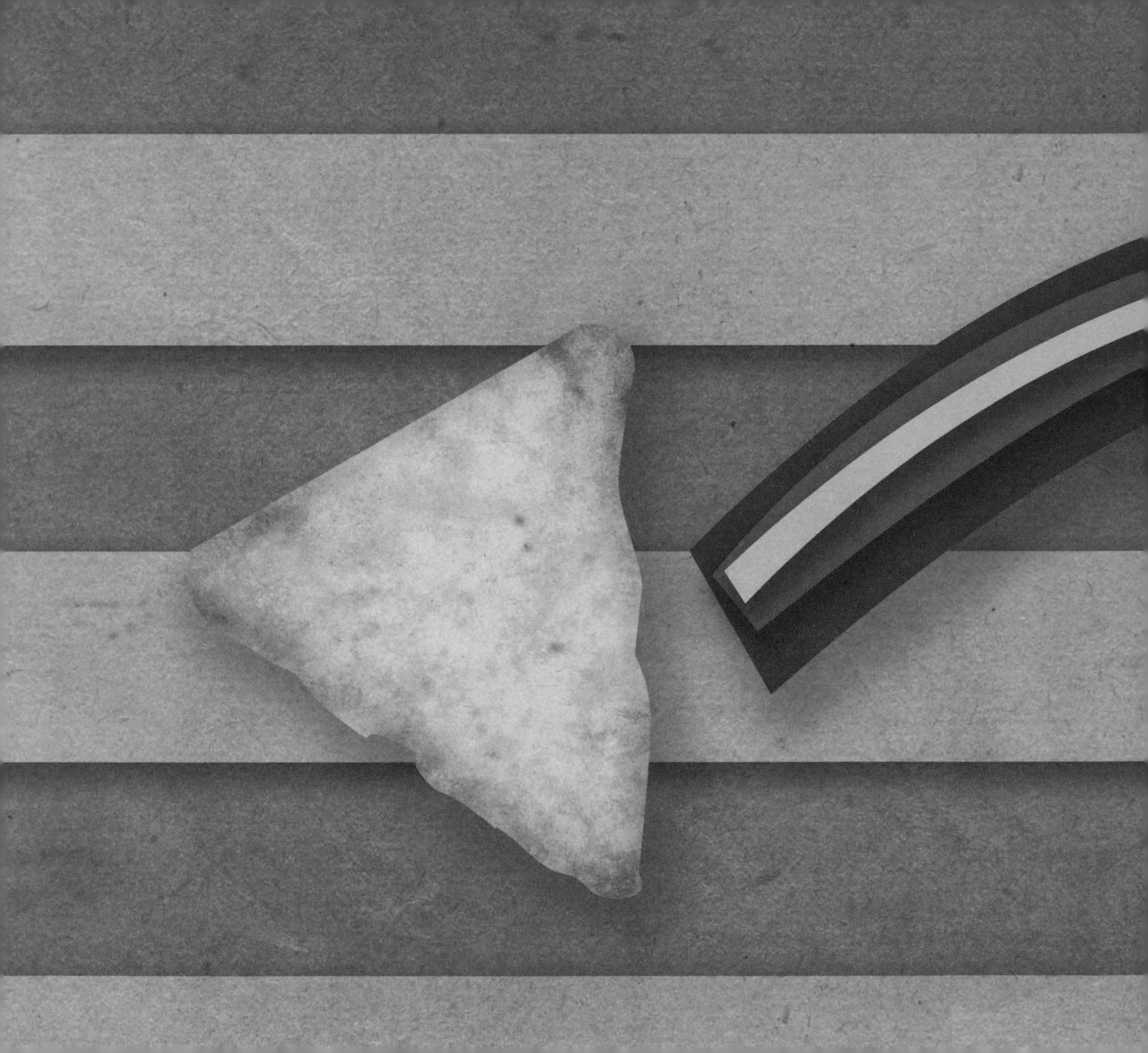

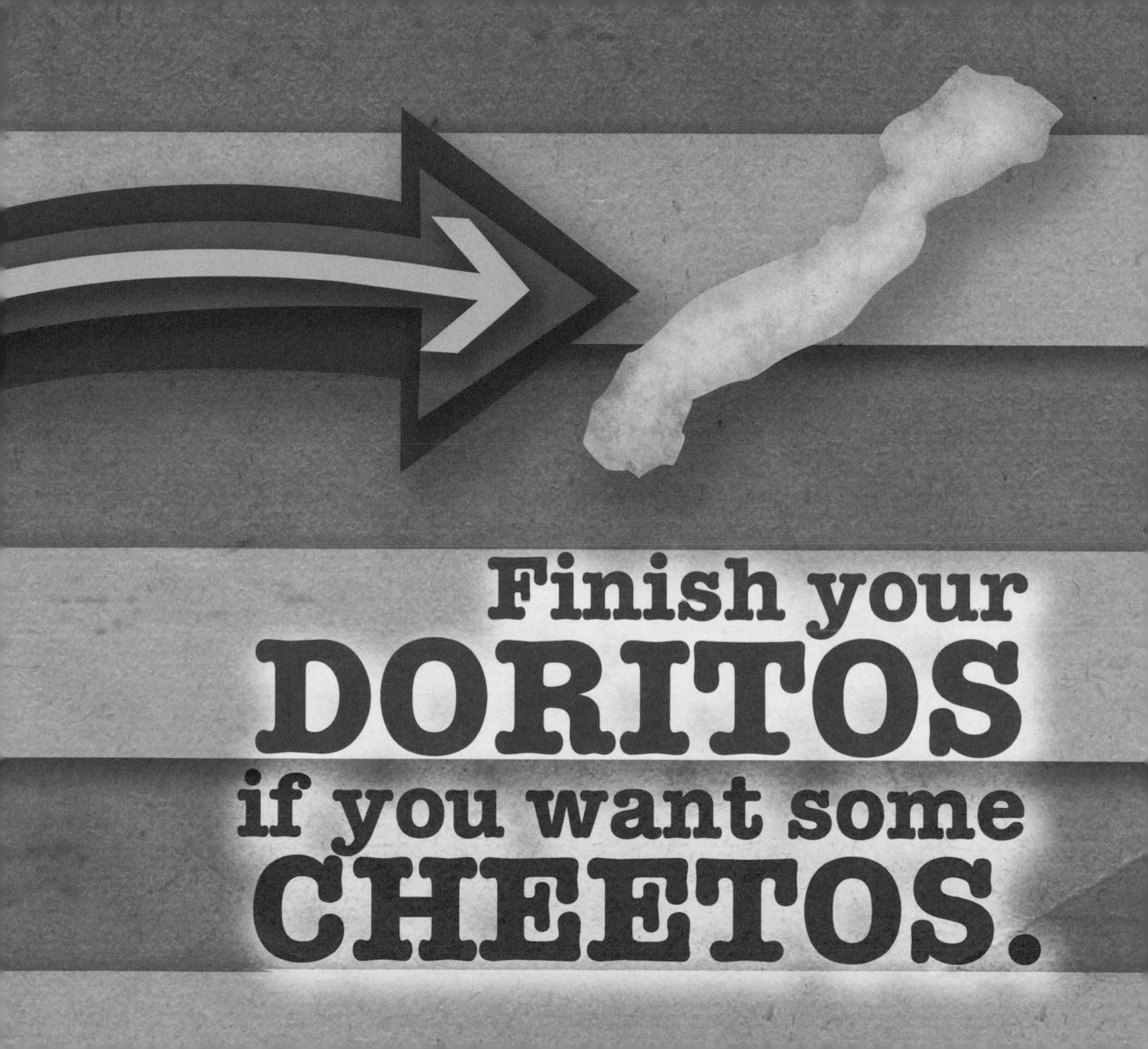
Finish your
DORITOS
if you want some
CHEETOS.

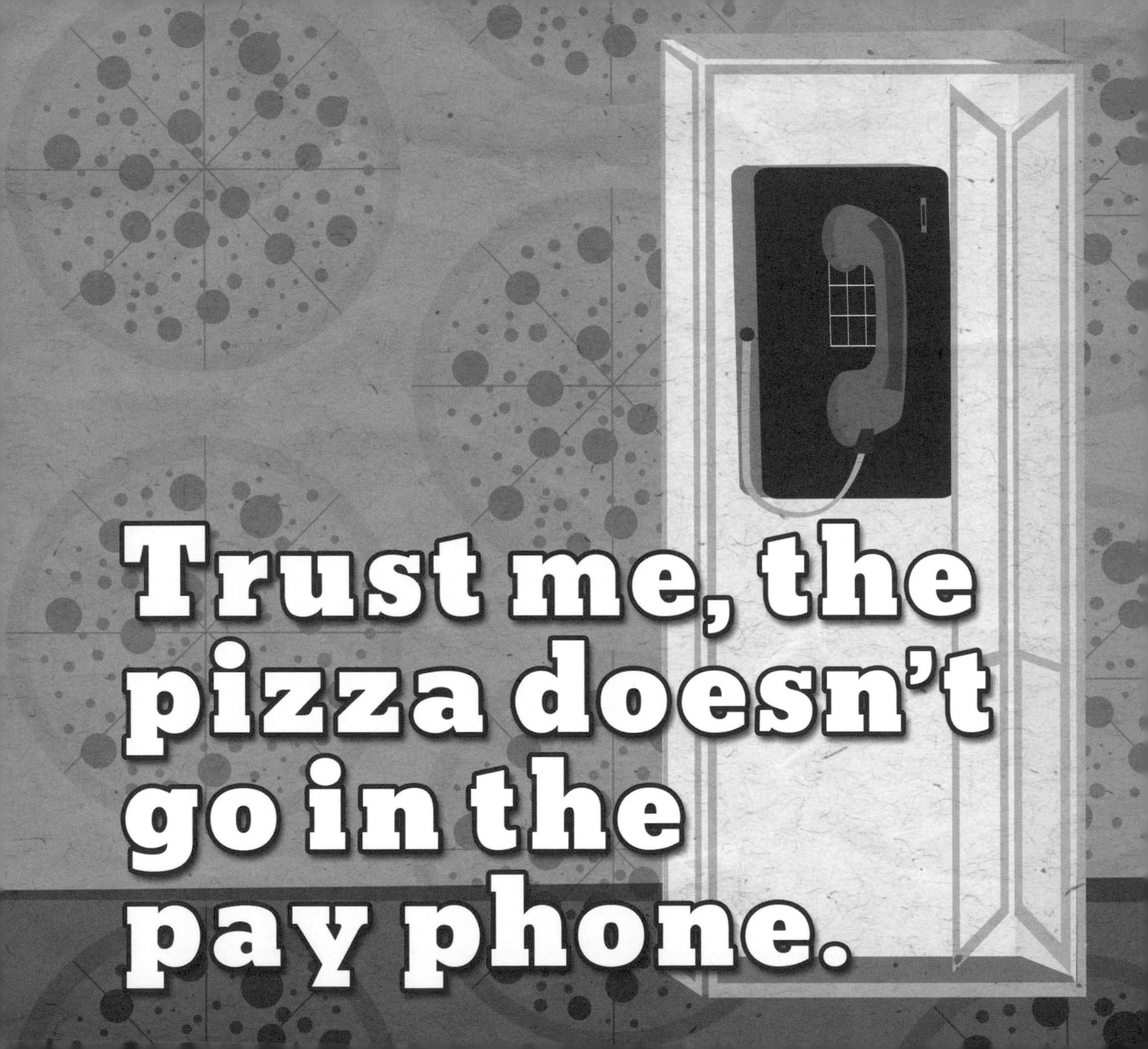

Trust me, the pizza doesn't go in the pay phone.

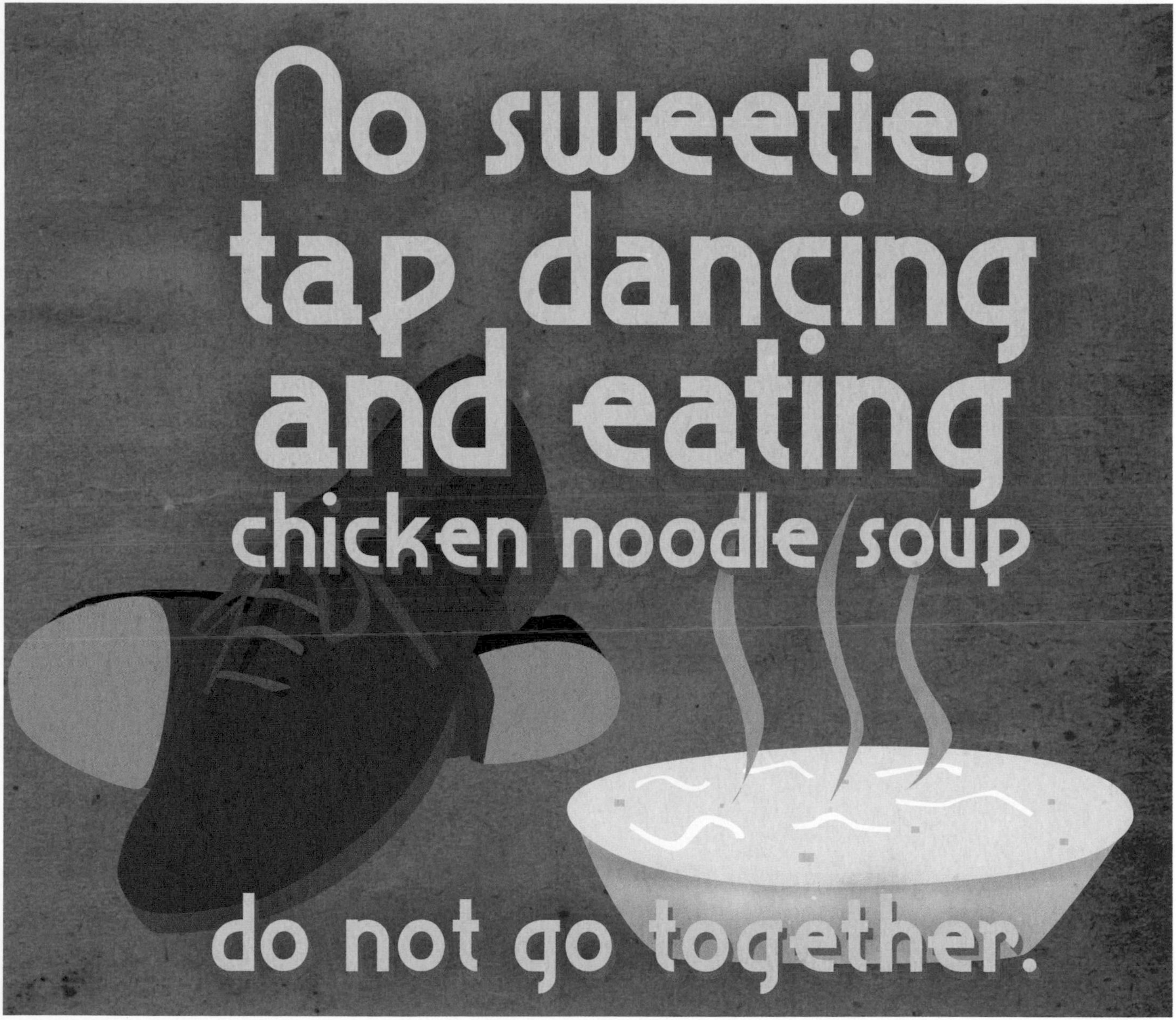
No sweetie,
tap dancing
and eating
chicken noodle soup
do not go together.

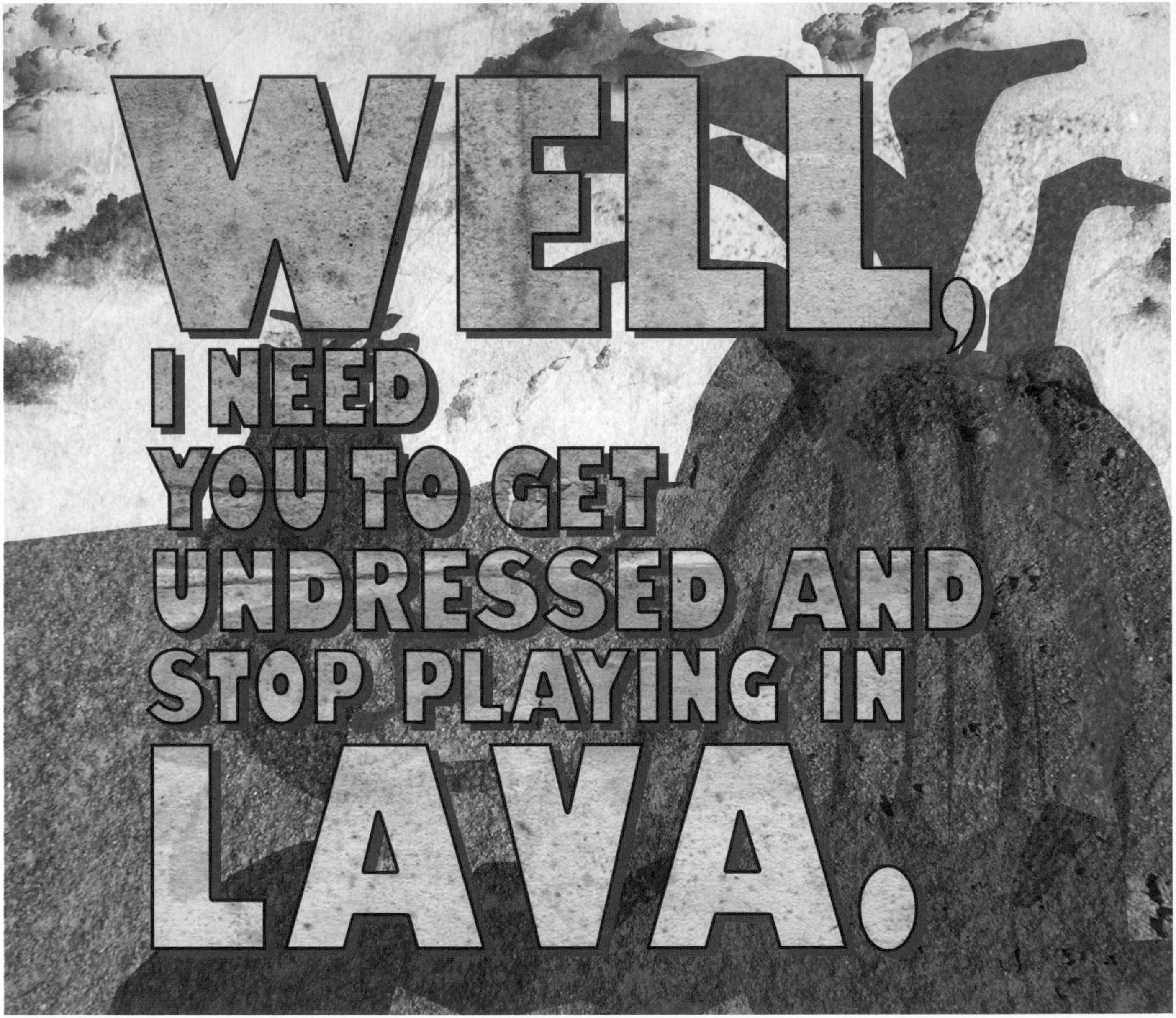
WELL,
I NEED
YOU TO GET
UNDRESSED AND
STOP PLAYING IN
LAVA.

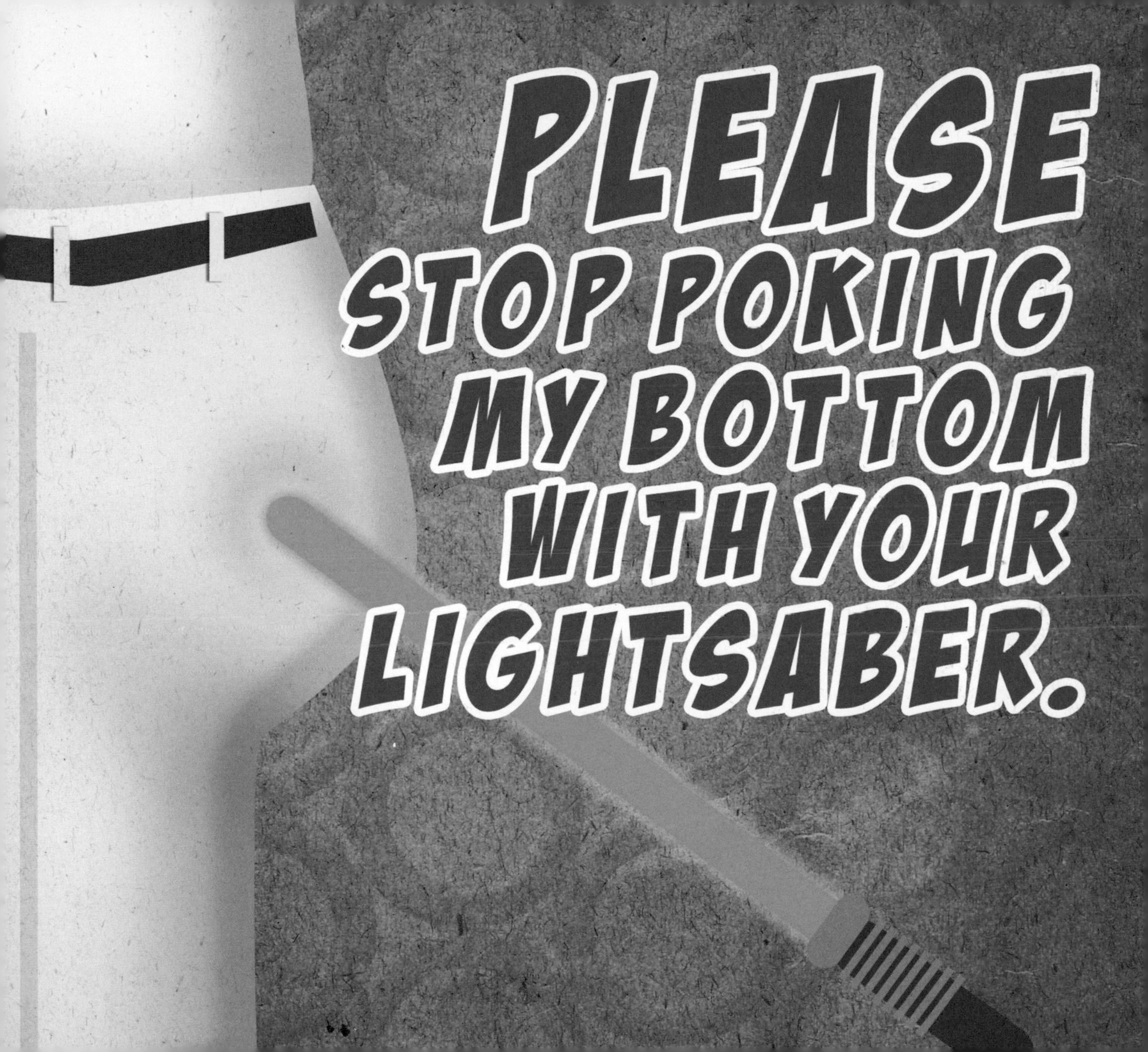
PLEASE
STOP POKING
MY BOTTOM
WITH YOUR
LIGHTSABER.

Let's not paint with milk.

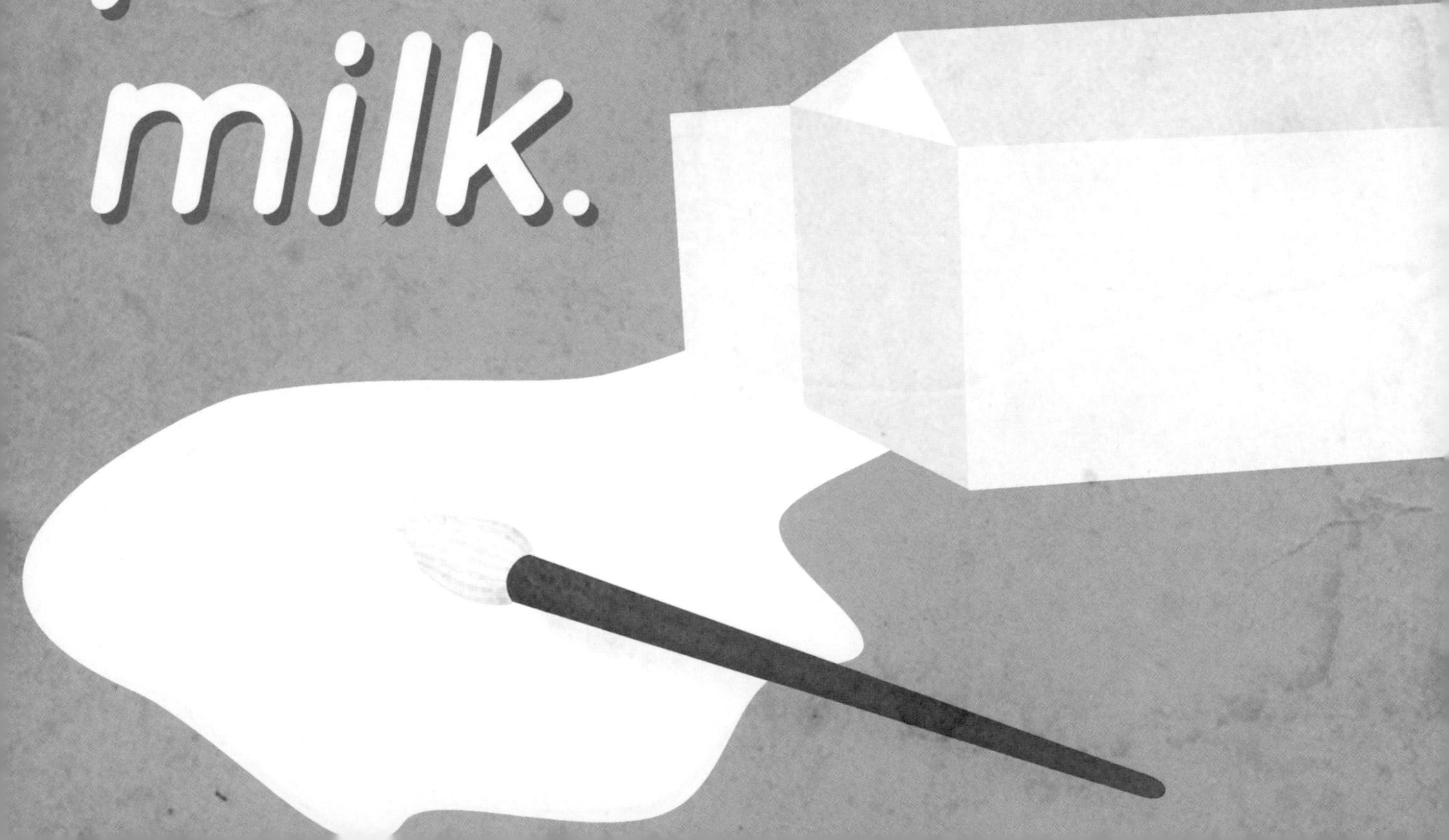

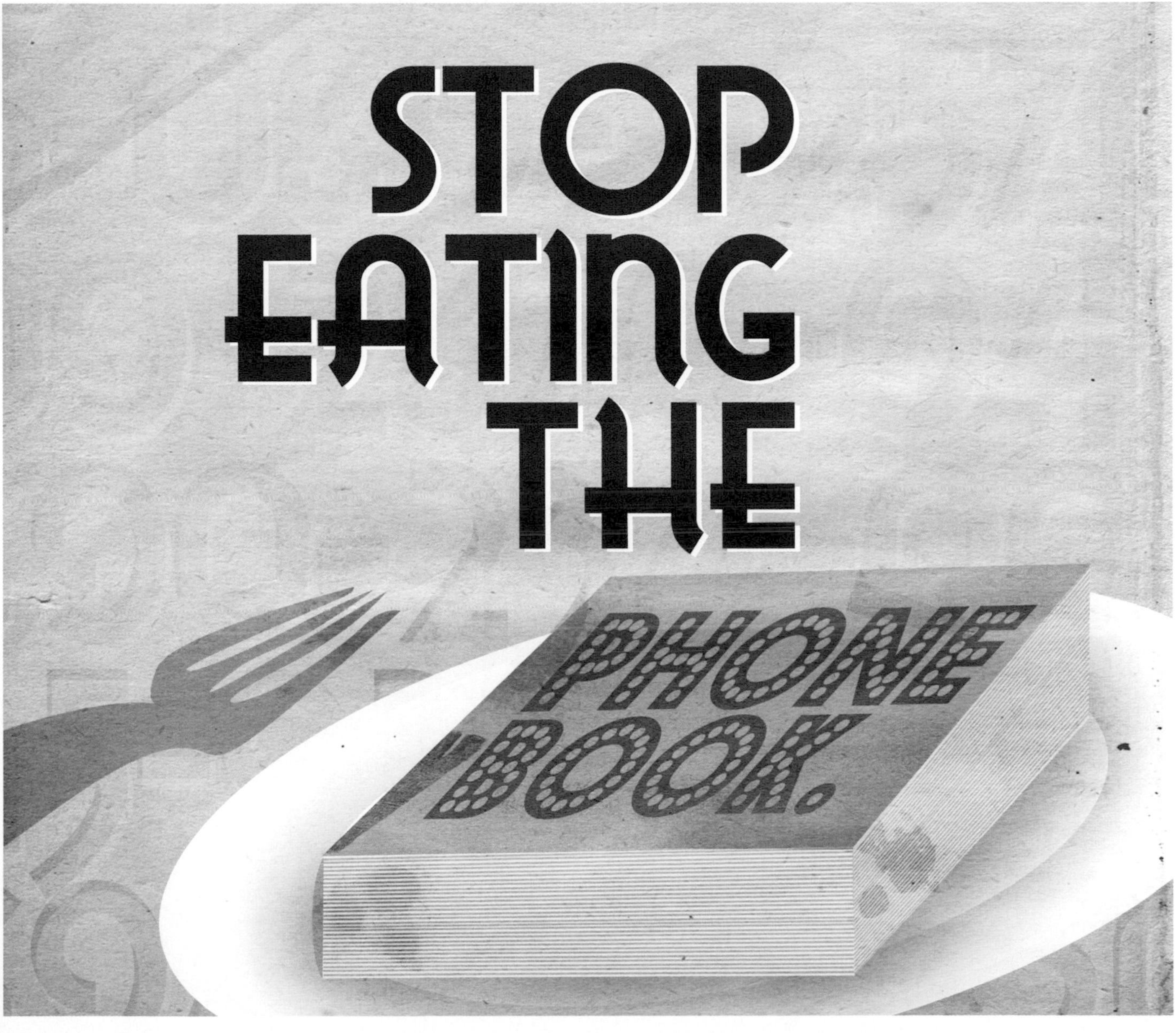
STOP
EATING
THE
PHONE
BOOK.

SUPERHEROES DON'T THROW FRUIT.

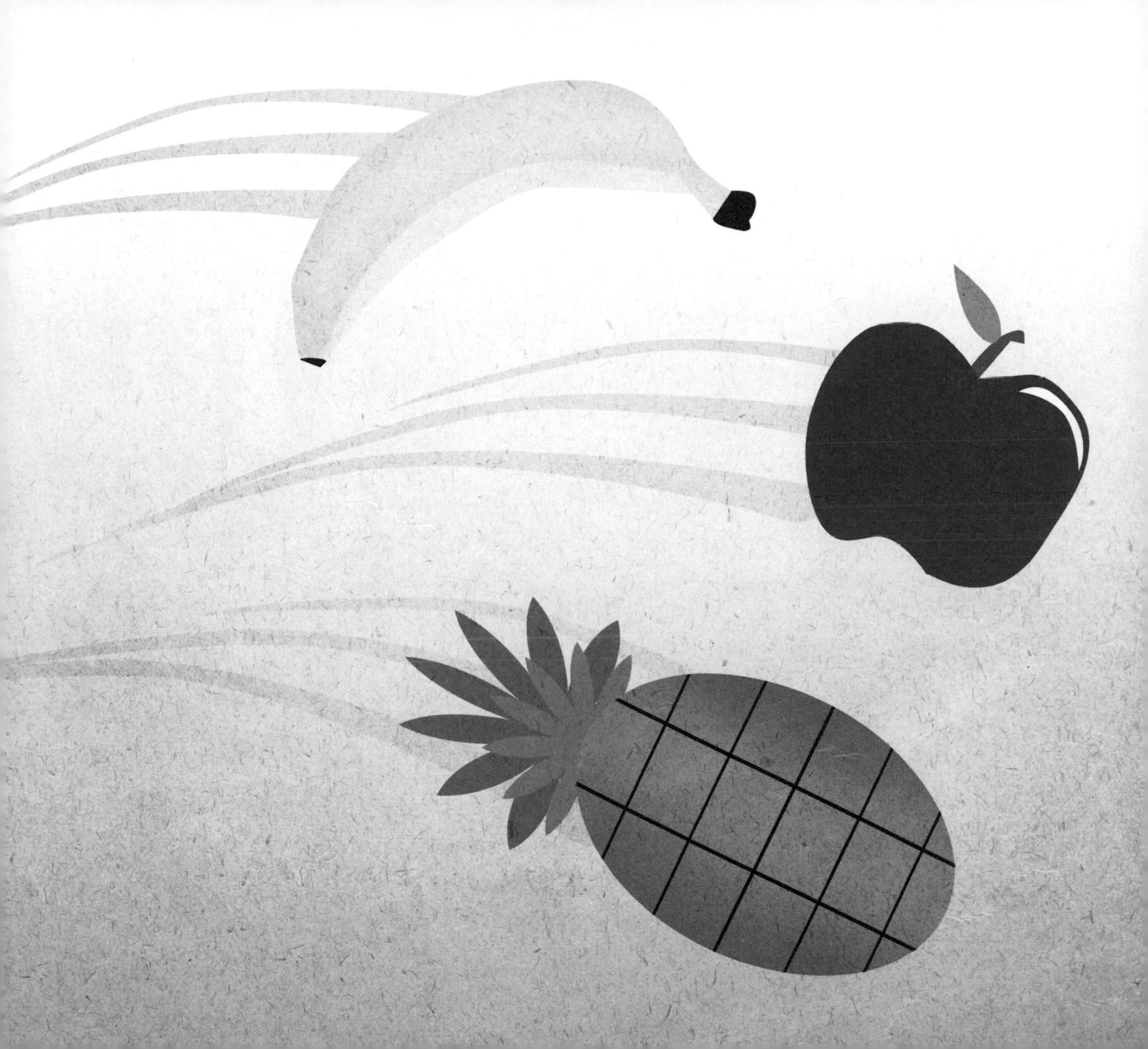

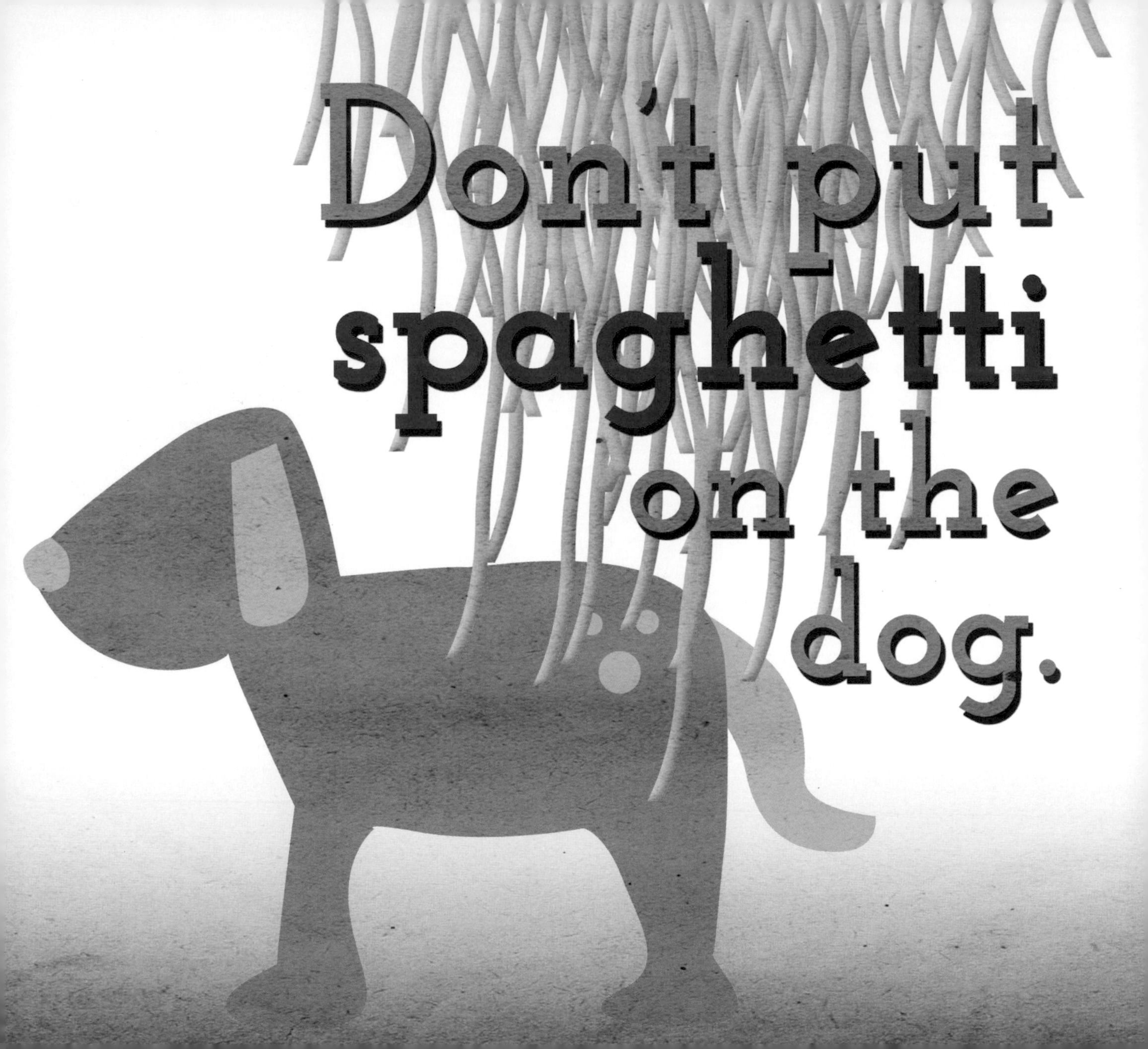

Don't put spaghetti on the dog.

YOU CAN'T GO AROUND STICKING CRAYONS IN OTHER PEOPLE'S EARS.

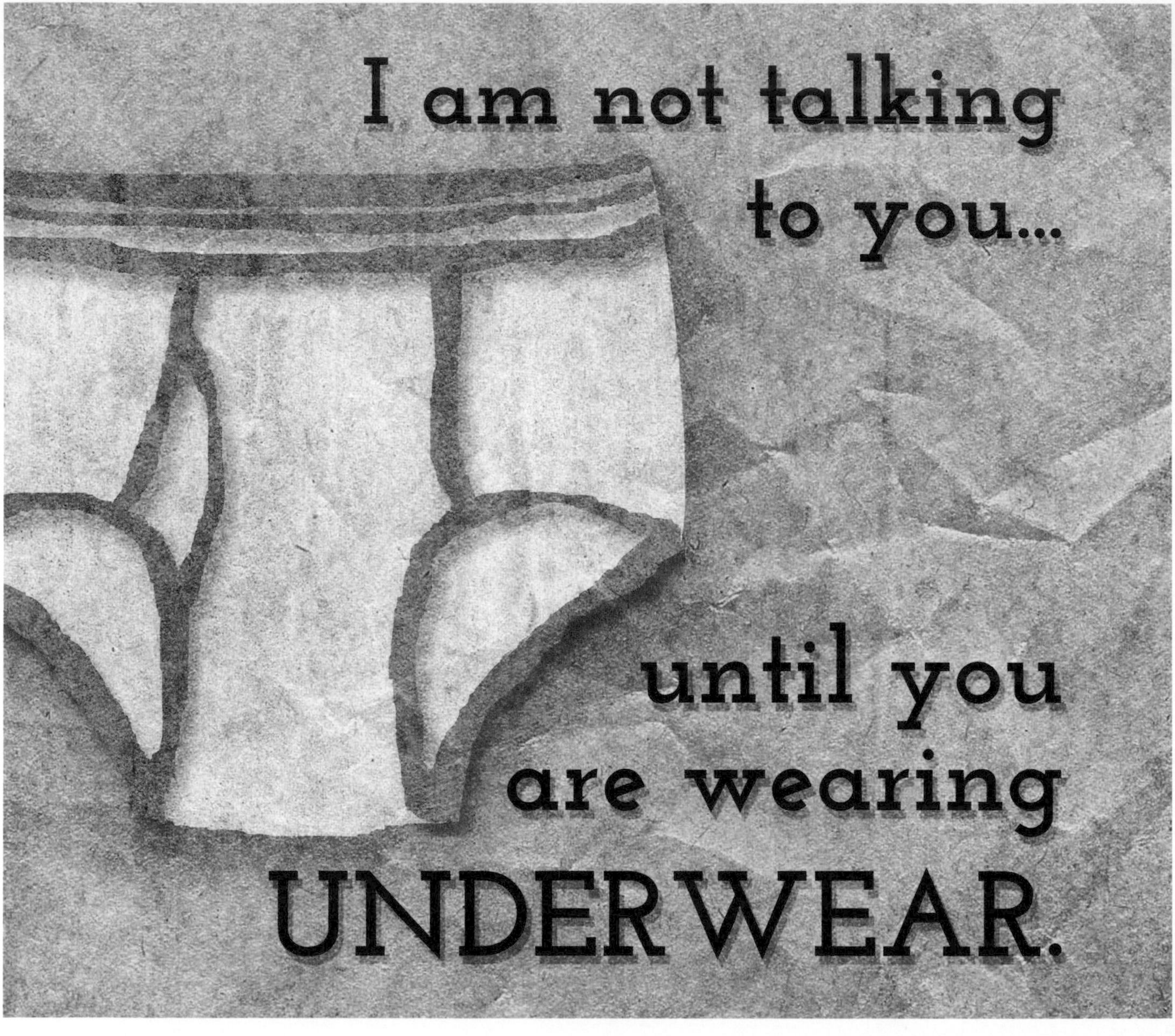
I am not talking
to you...
until you
are wearing
UNDERWEAR.

Dont kiss your brother while he is on the toilet.

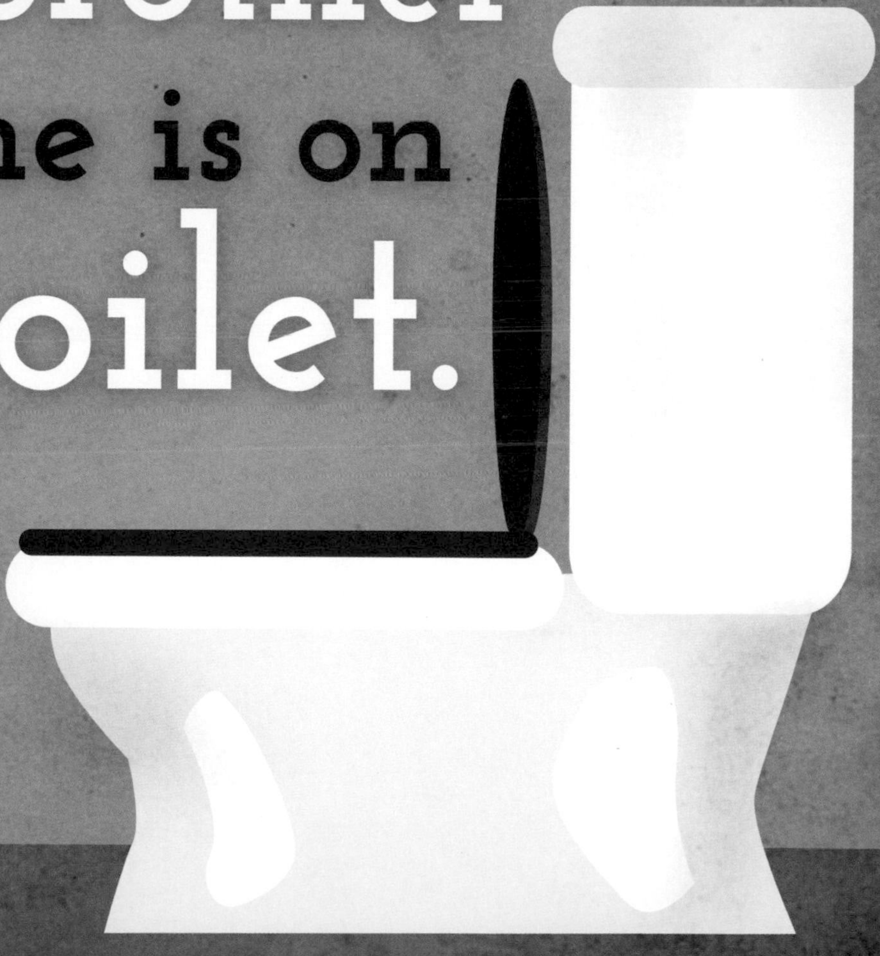

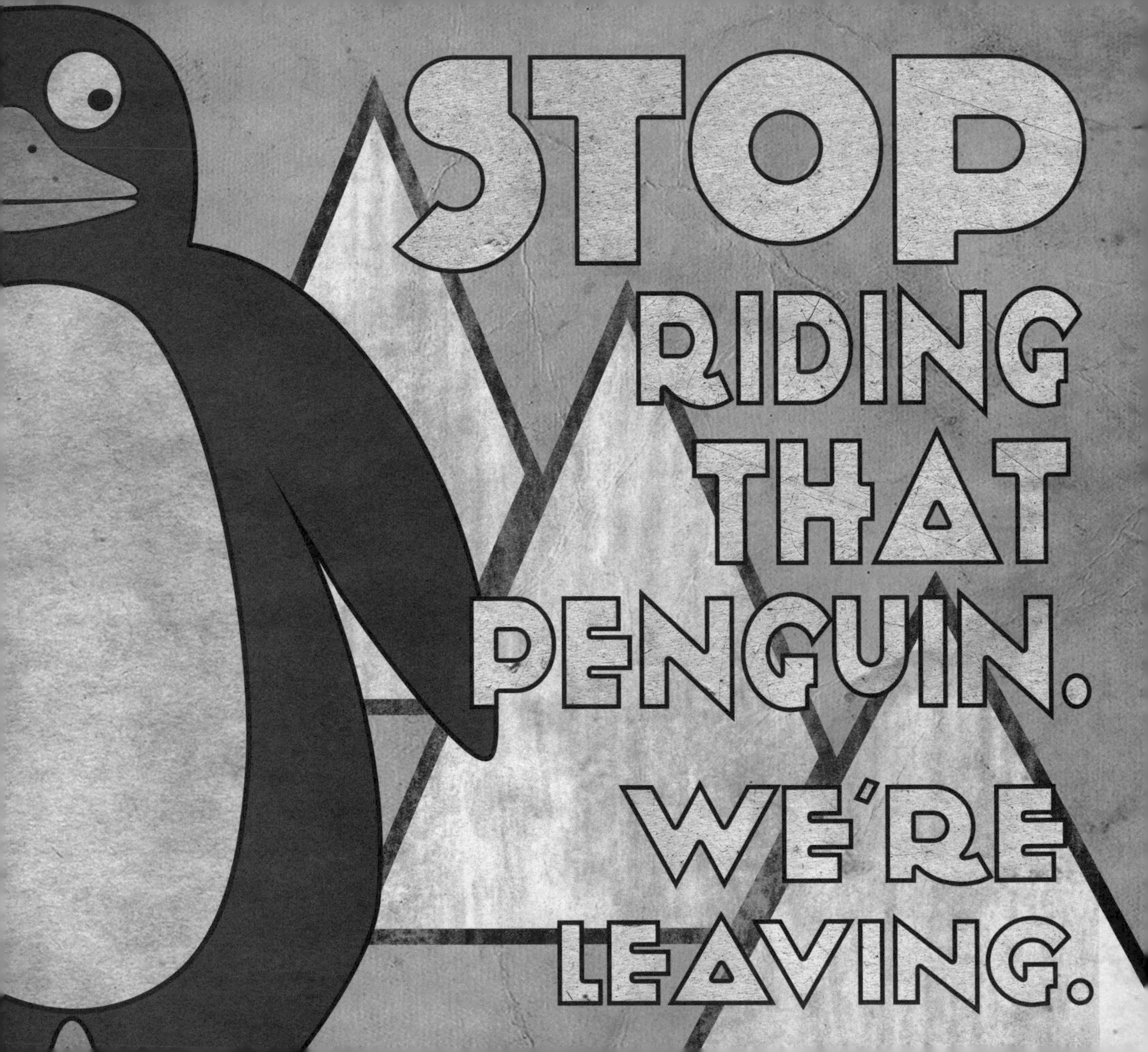
STOP
RIDING
THAT
PENGUIN.
WE'RE
LEAVING.

DON'T

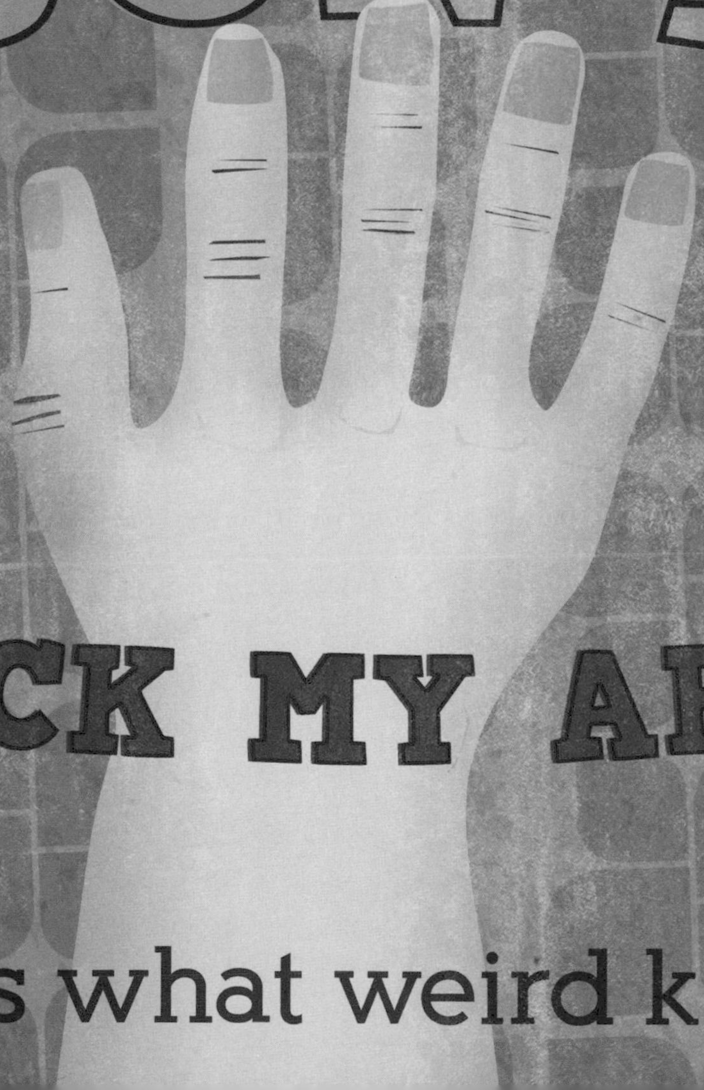

LICK MY ARM!

That's what weird kids do.

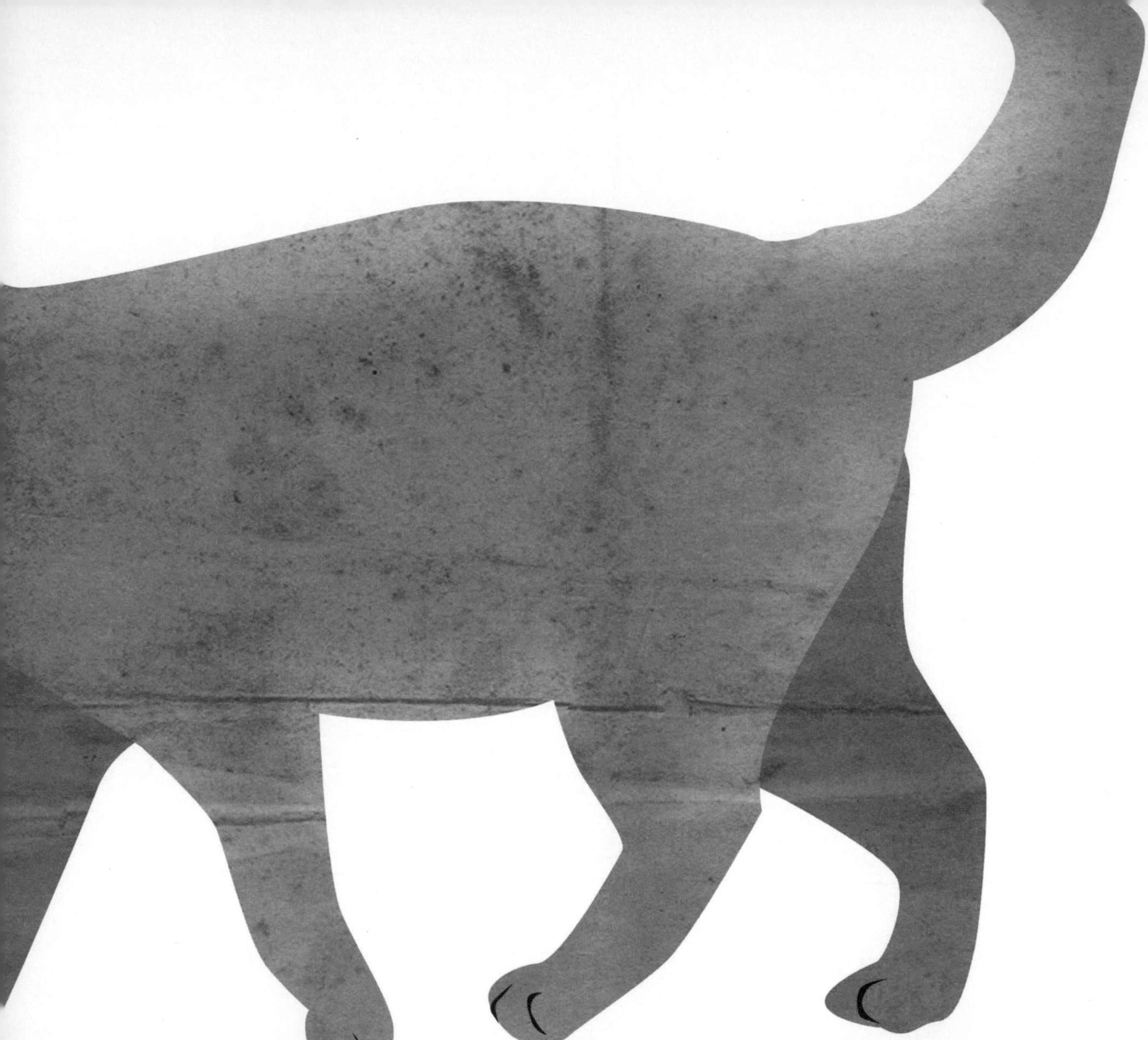

THE CAT DOES NOT WANT TO WEAR LIPSTICK.

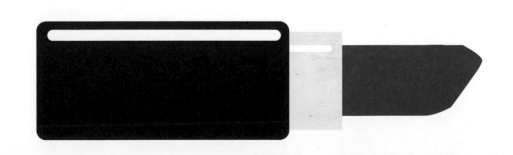

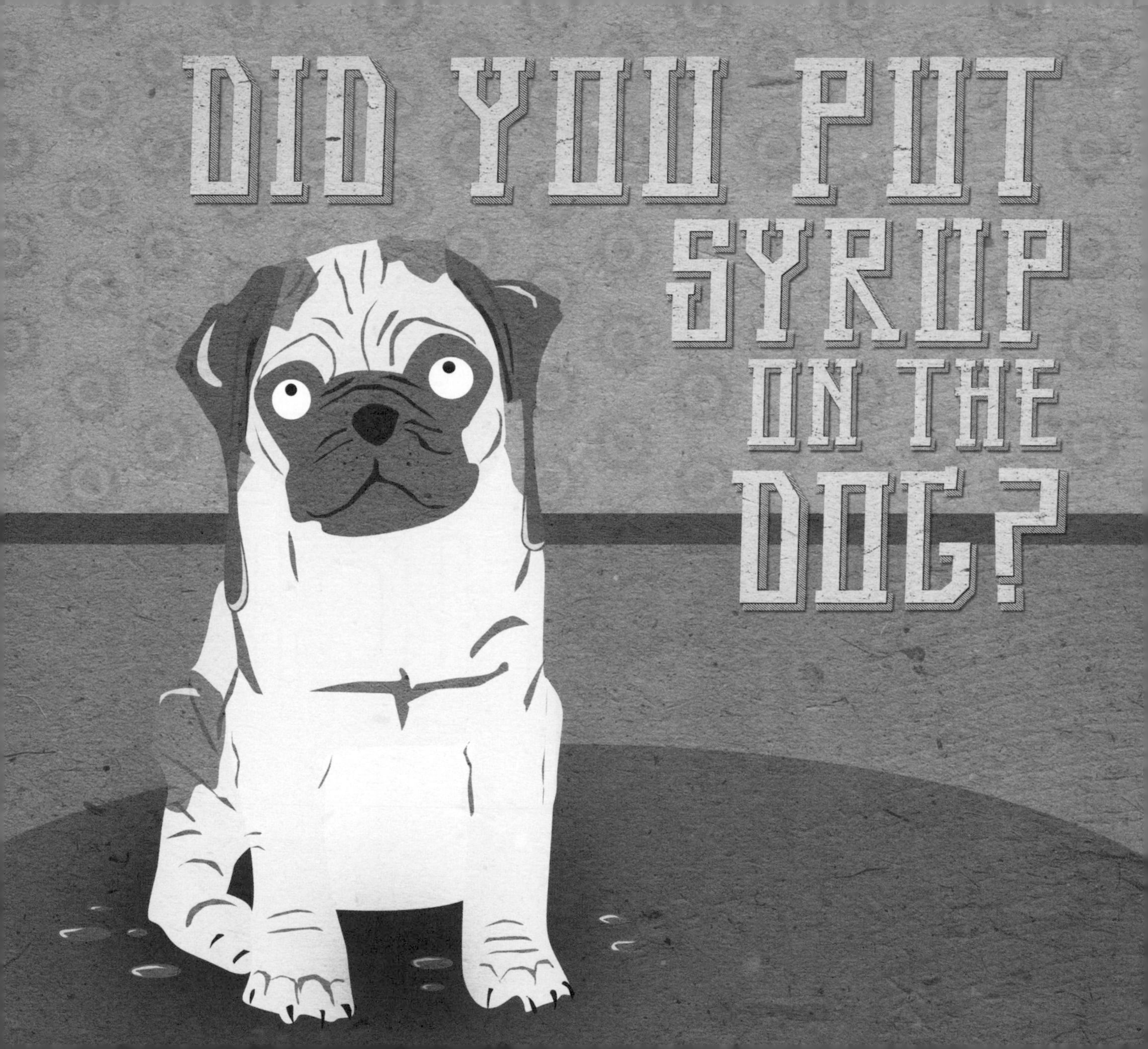
DID YOU PUT SYRUP ON THE DOG?

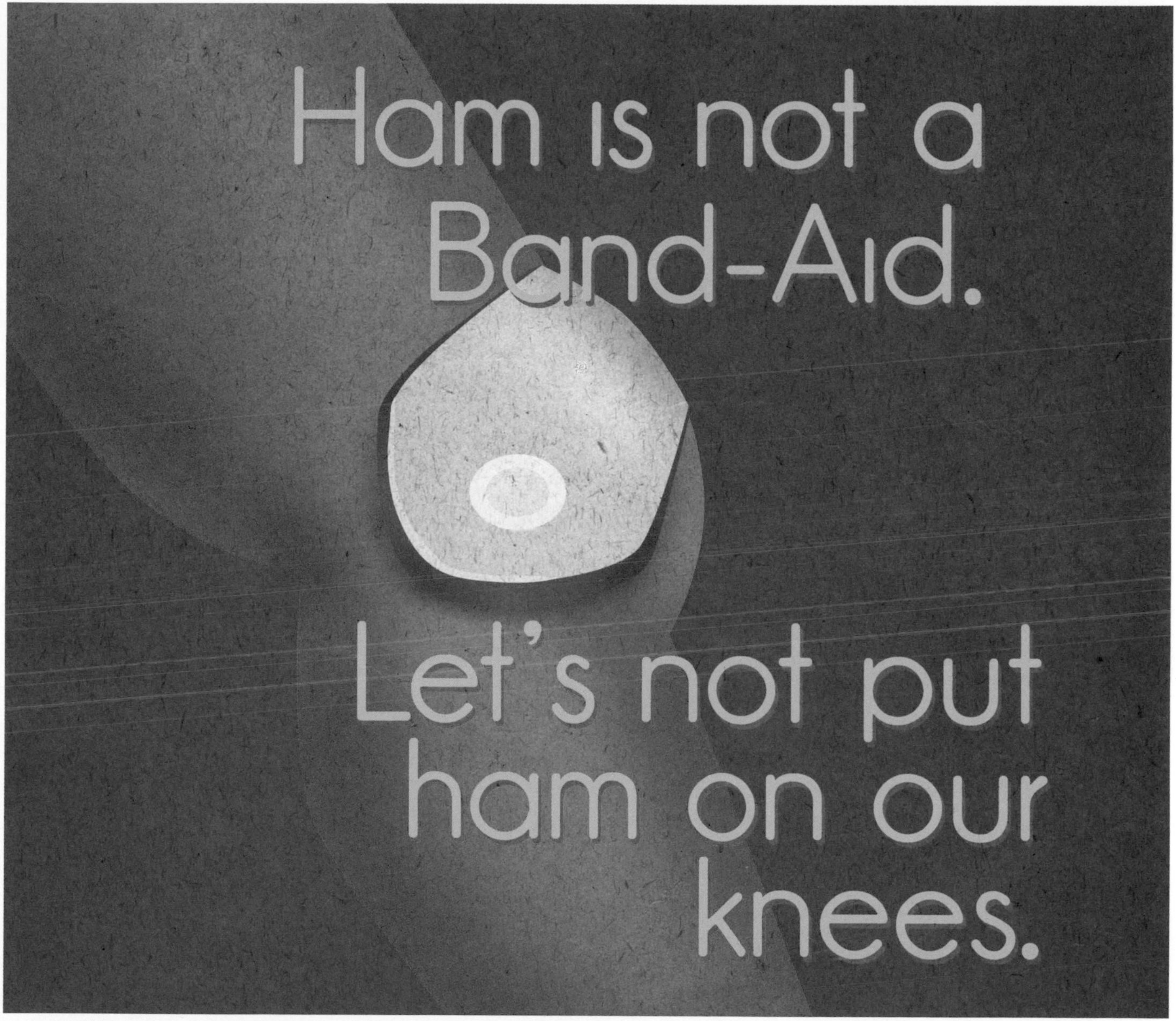

Ham is not a Band-Aid.

Let's not put ham on our knees.

PLEASE DON'T EAT THE GOLDFISH CRACKERS YOU'VE PUT IN YOUR BUTT.

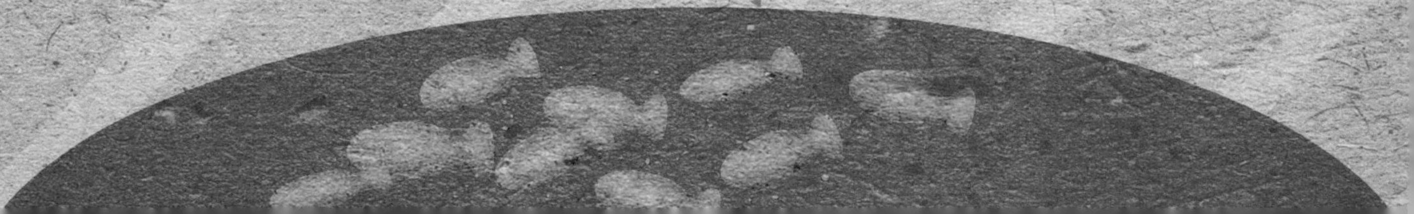

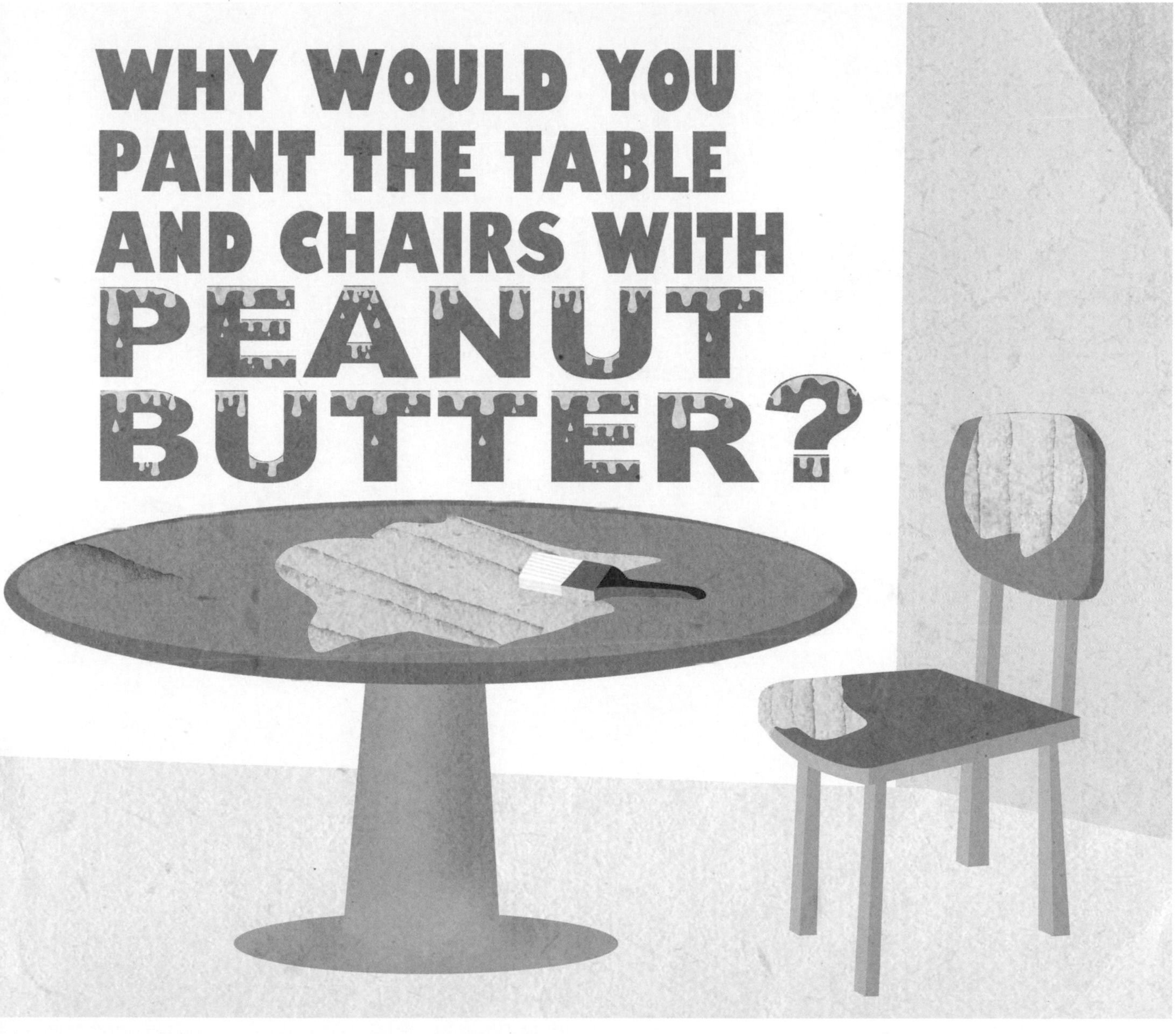
WHY WOULD YOU PAINT THE TABLE AND CHAIRS WITH PEANUT BUTTER?

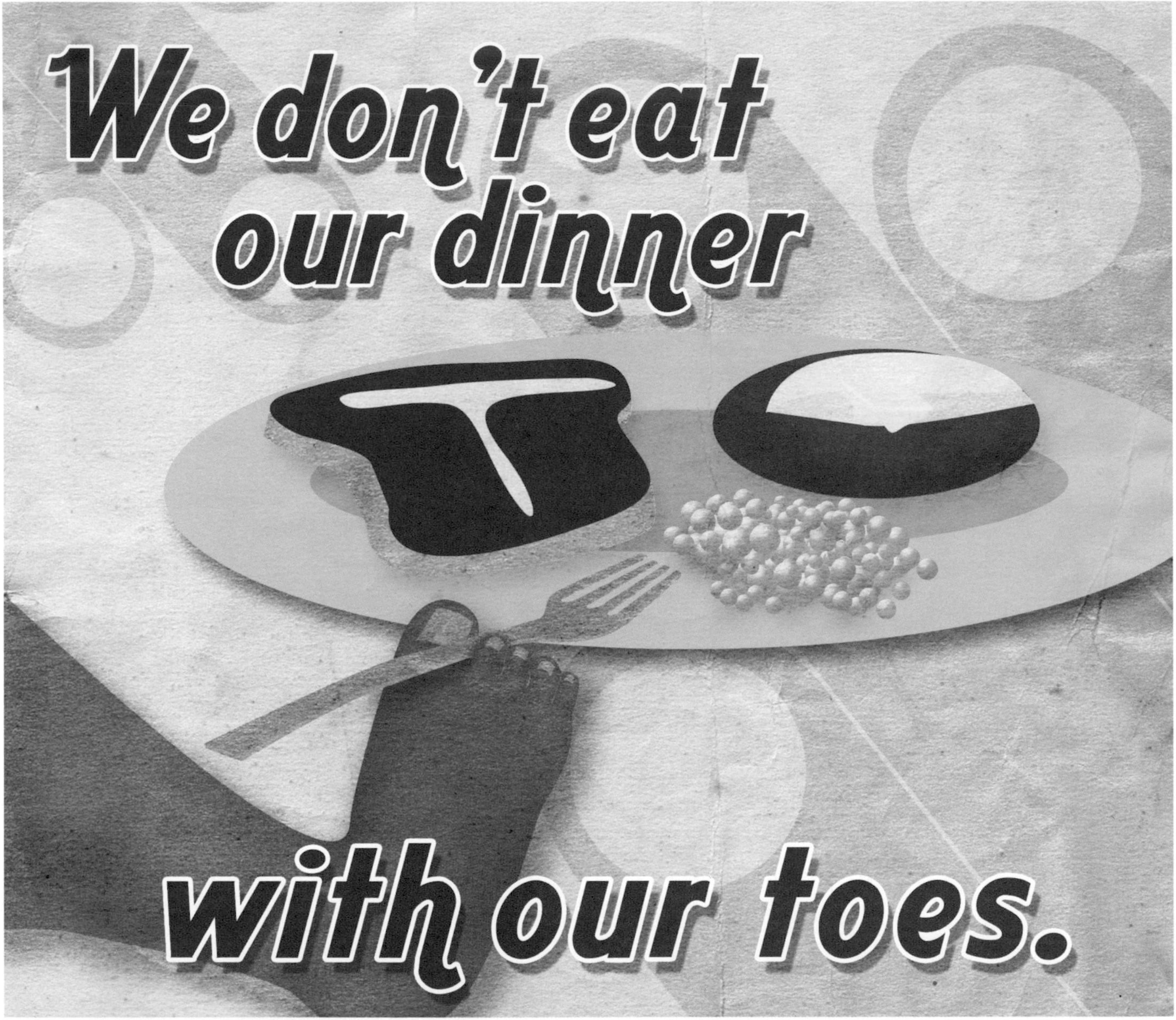
We don't eat
our dinner
with our toes.

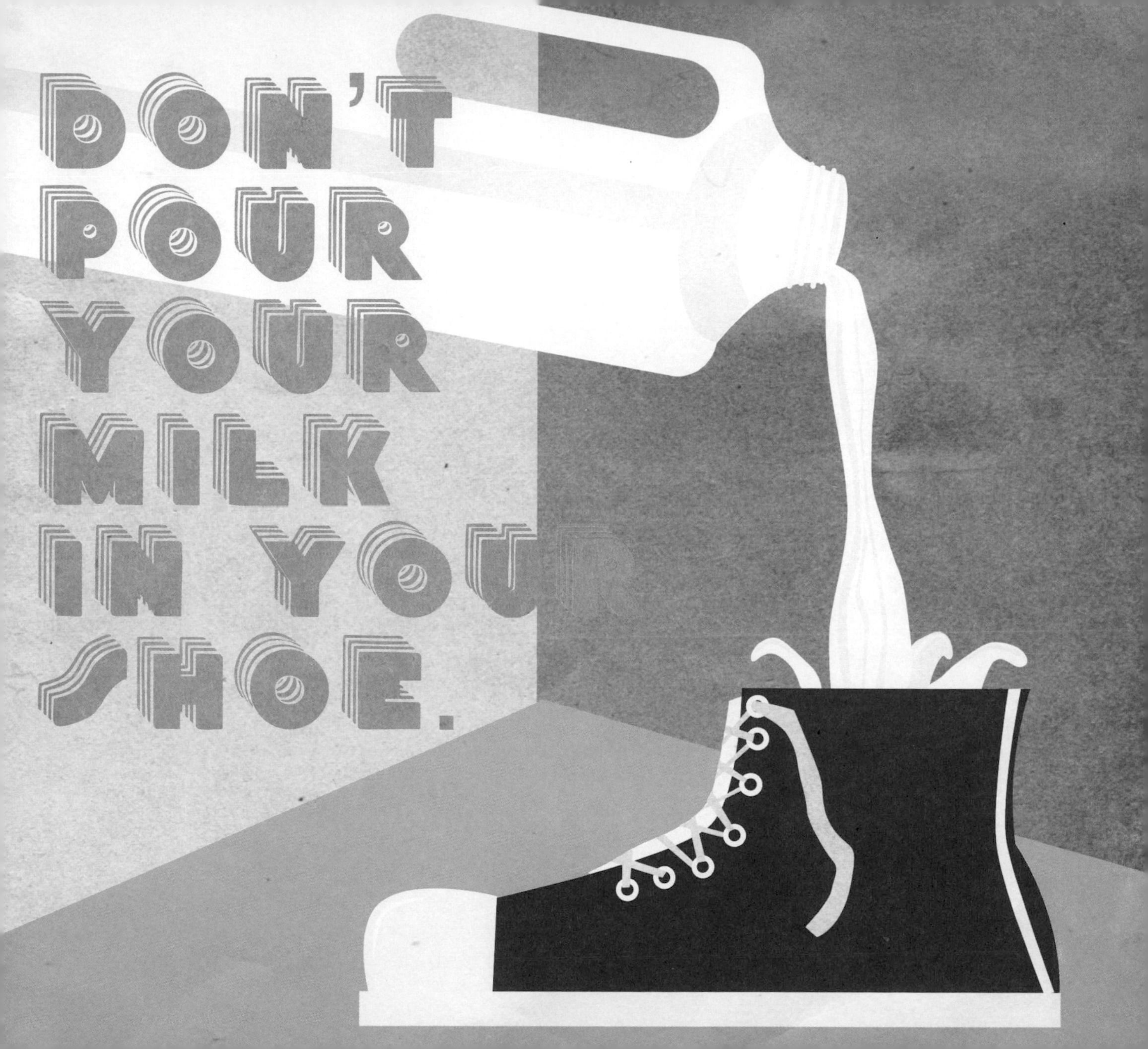
DON'T POUR YOUR MILK IN YOUR SHOE.

The dog is not a
jungle gym.

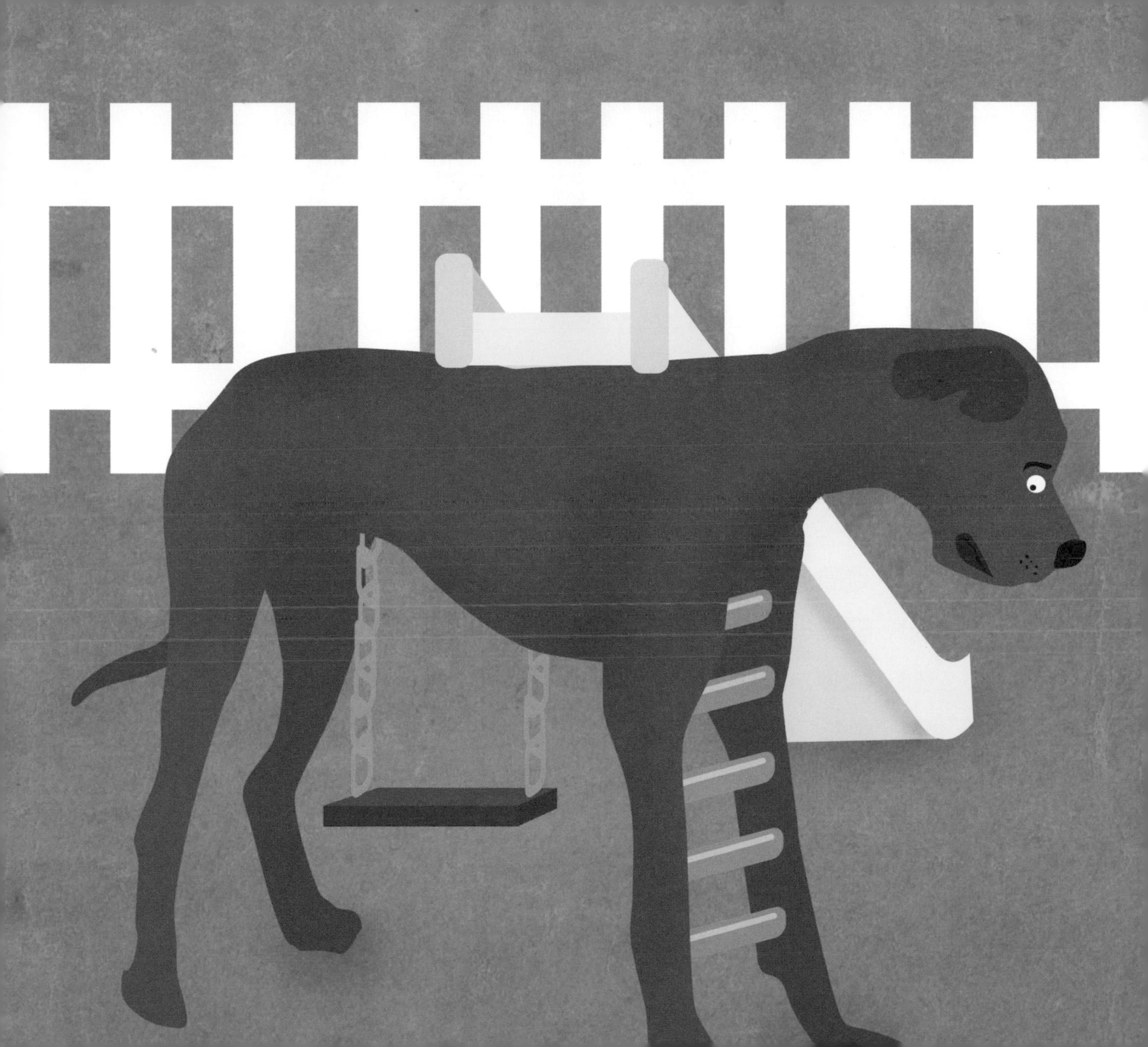

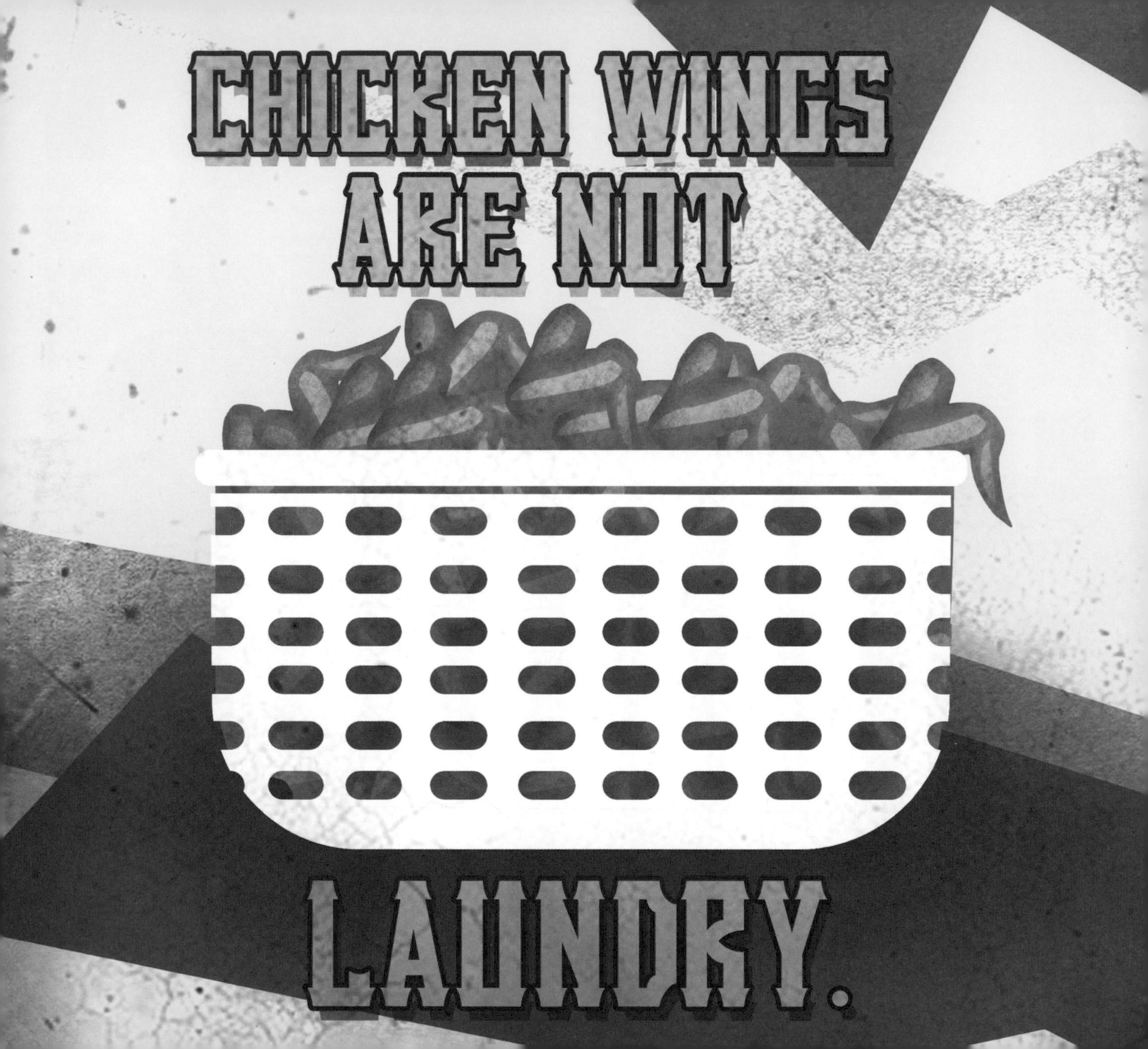
CHICKEN WINGS
ARE NOT
LAUNDRY.

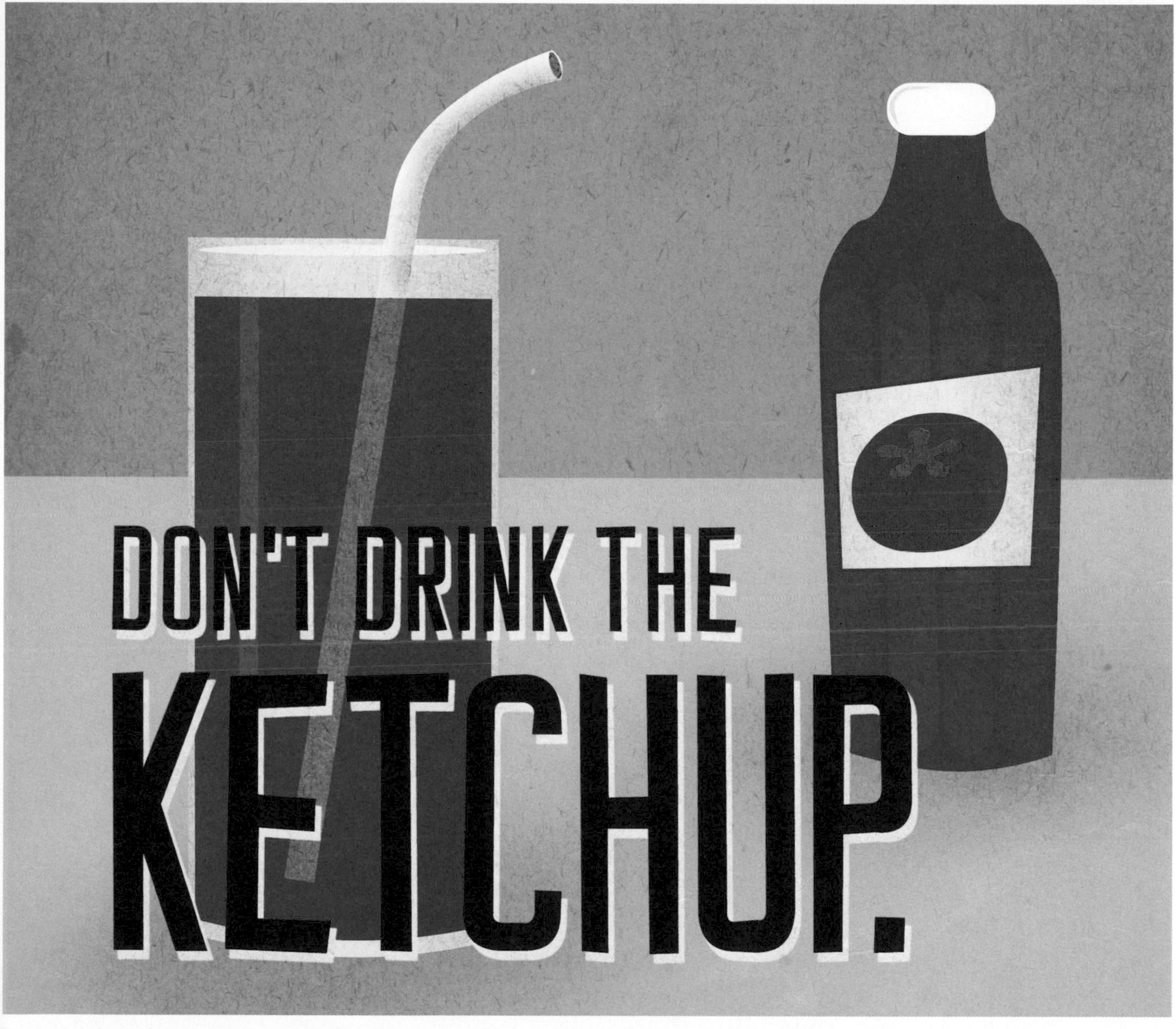
DON'T DRINK THE
KETCHUP.

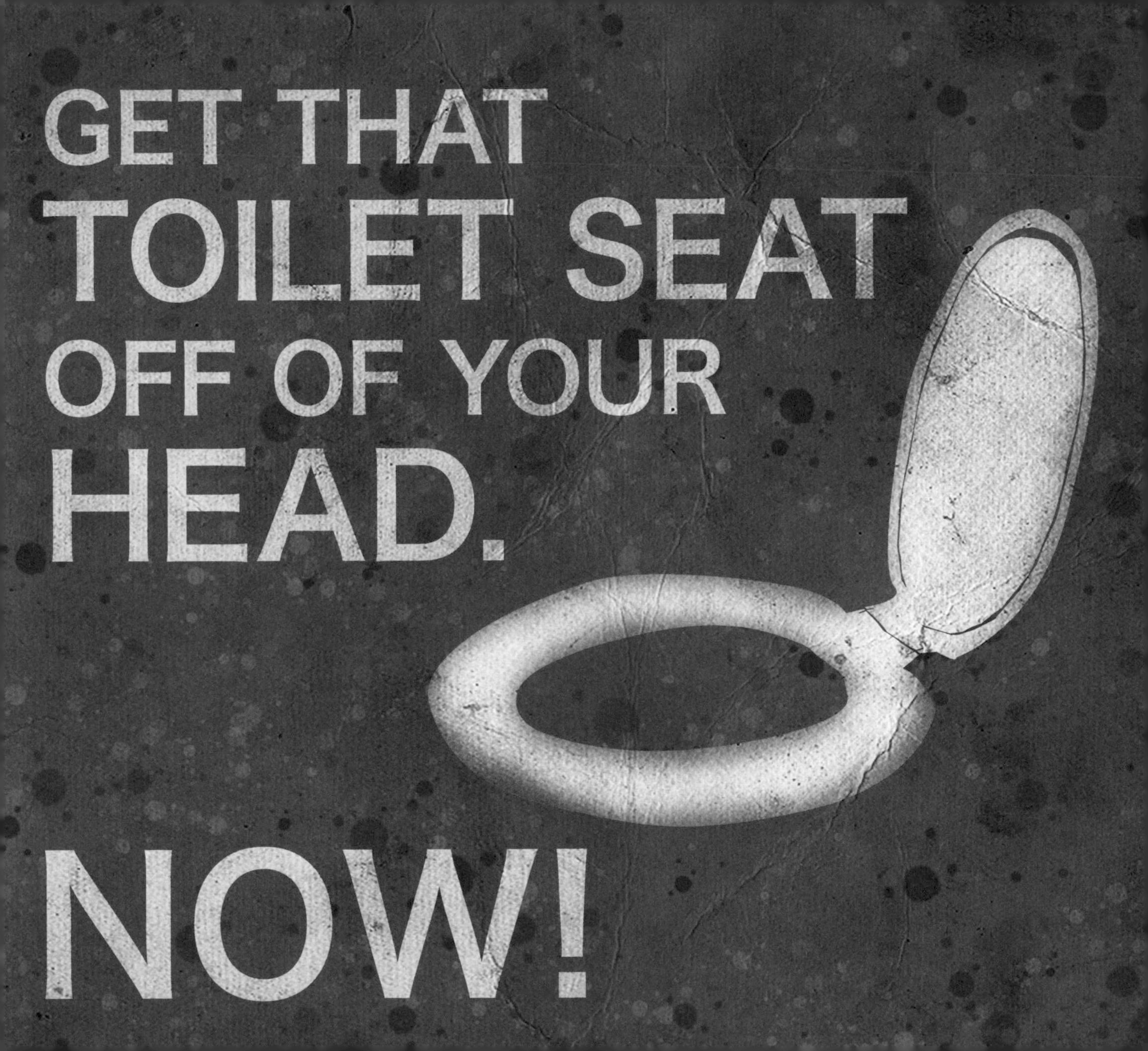
GET THAT
TOILET SEAT
OFF OF YOUR
HEAD.
NOW!

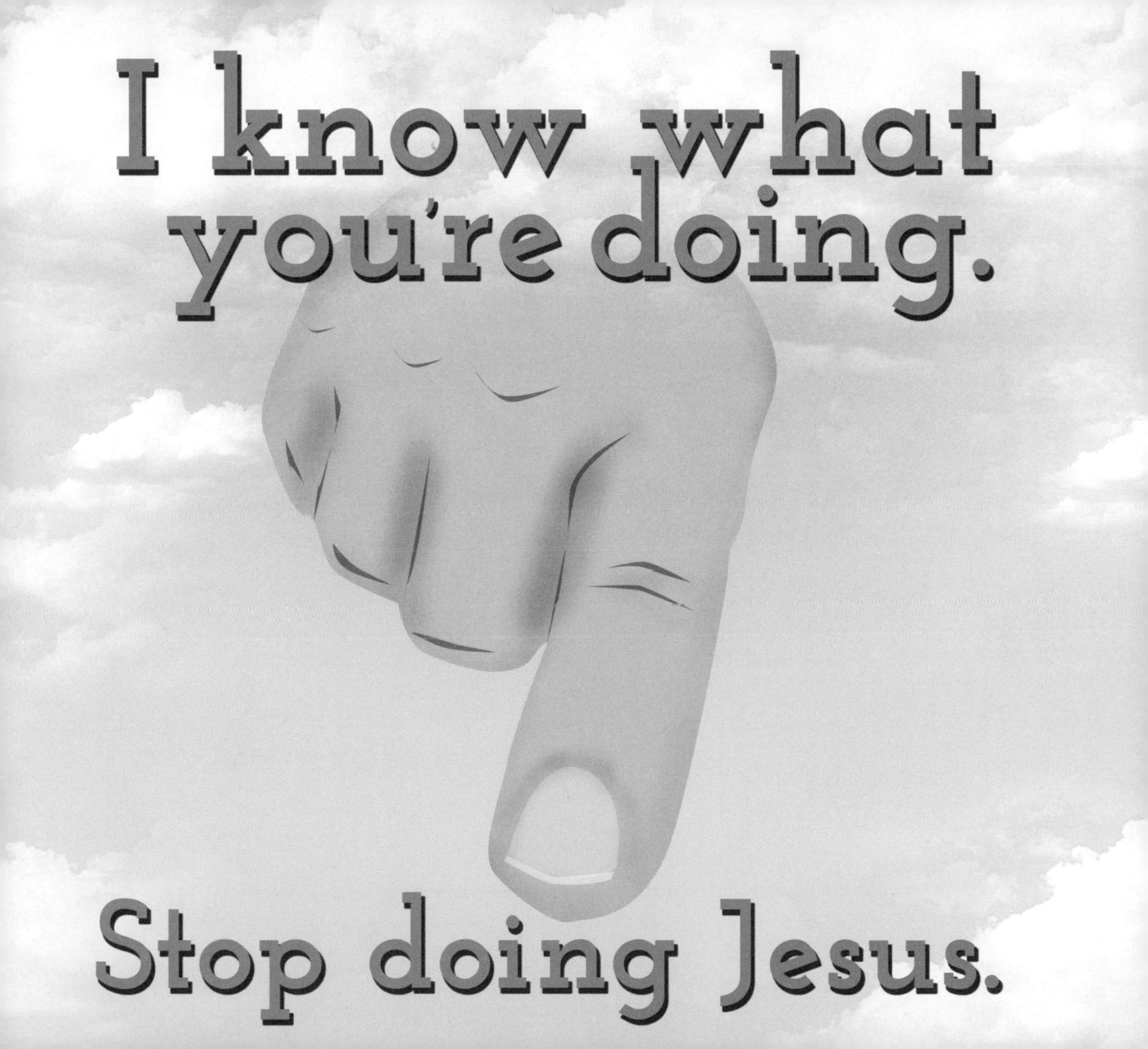

I know what you're doing.

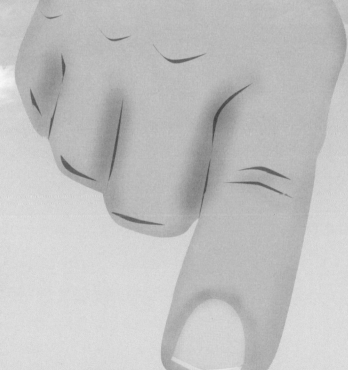

Stop doing Jesus.

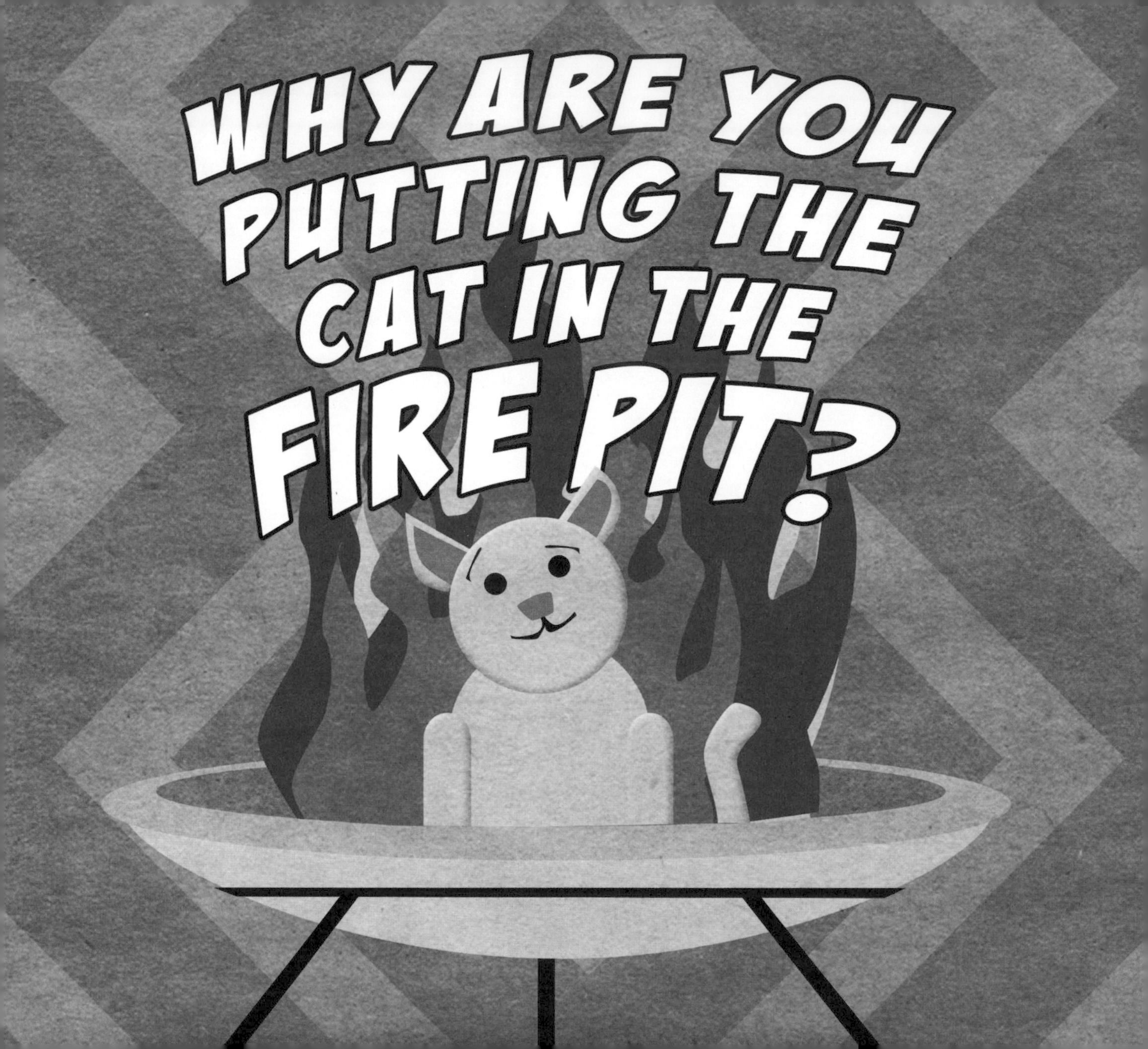
WHY ARE YOU PUTTING THE CAT IN THE FIRE PIT?

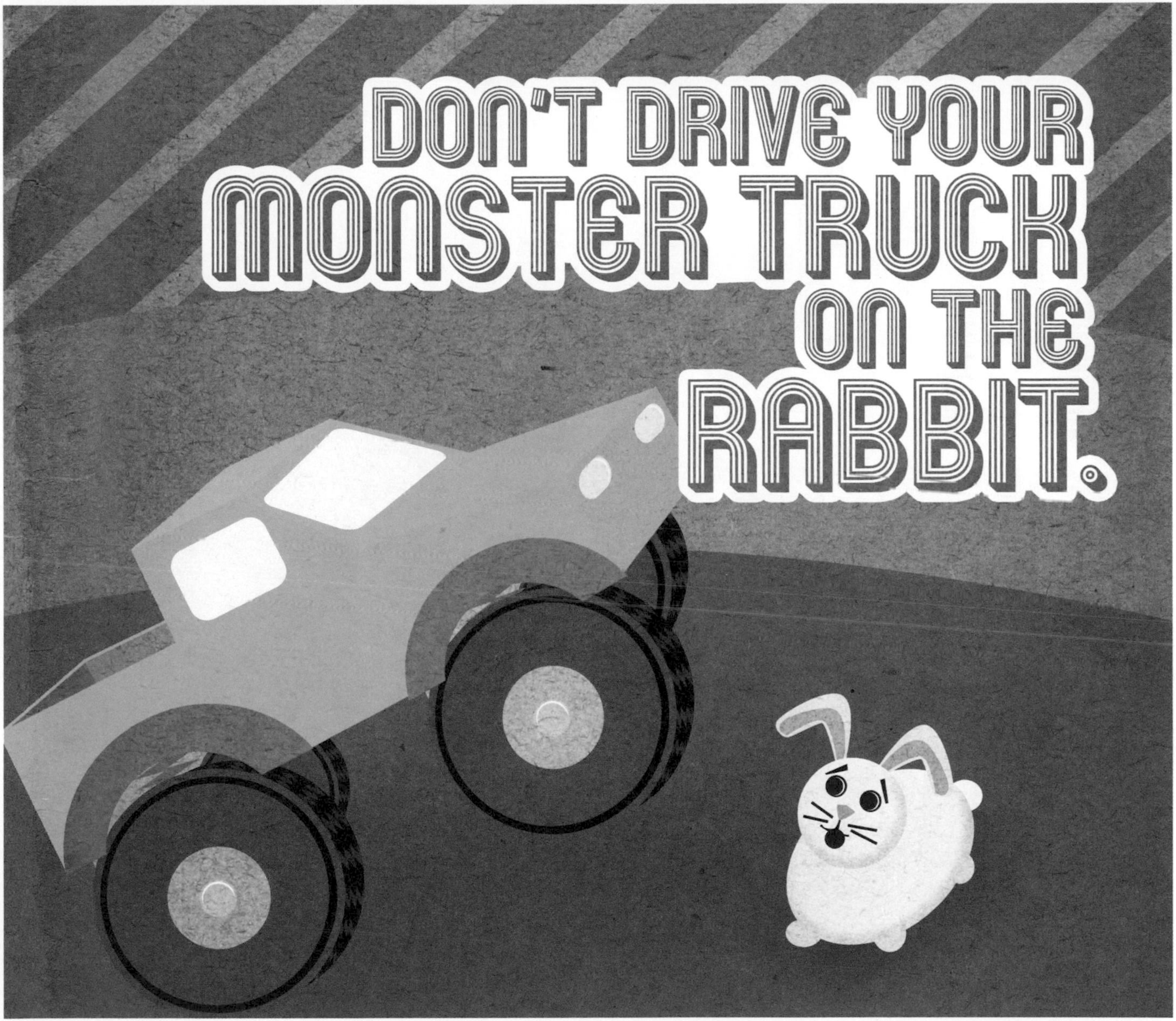
DON'T DRIVE YOUR
MONSTER TRUCK
ON THE
RABBIT.

Did you just KISS the monkey?

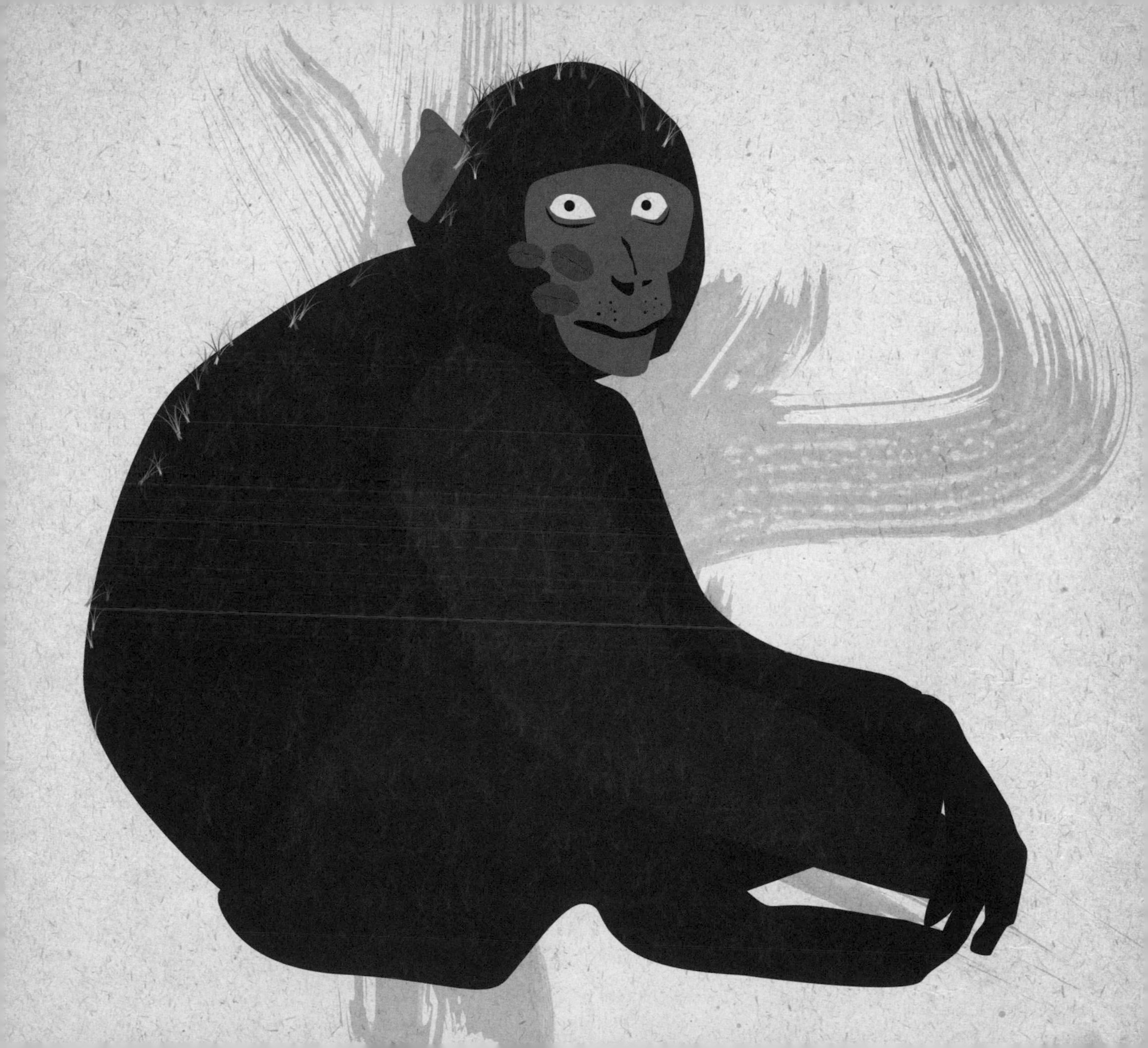

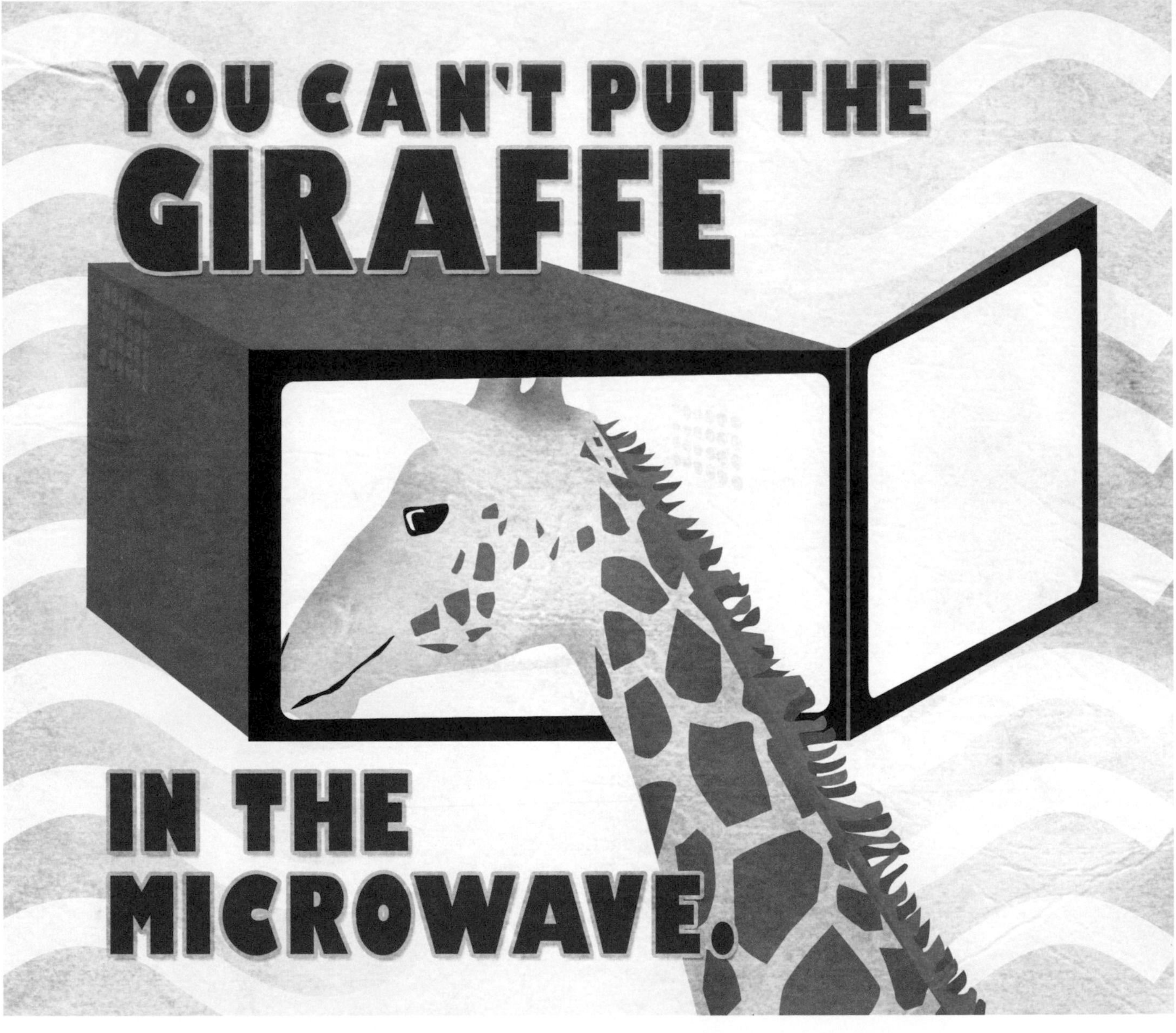
YOU CAN'T PUT THE
GIRAFFE
IN THE
MICROWAVE.

Don't put the zebra in the blender.

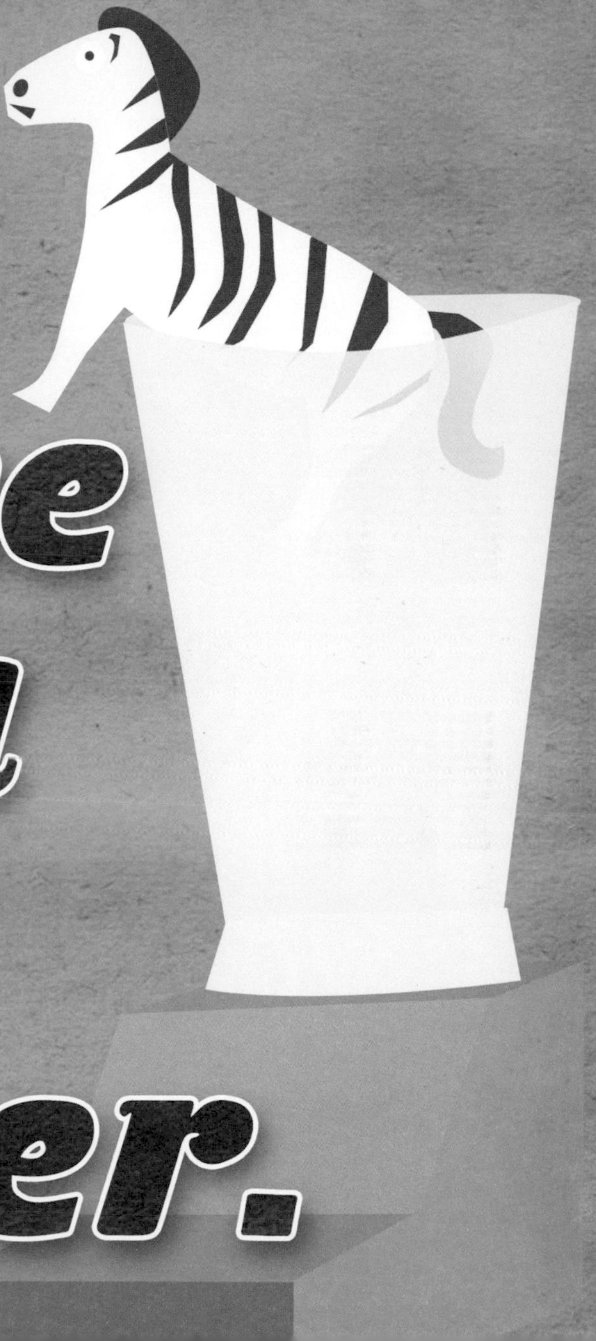

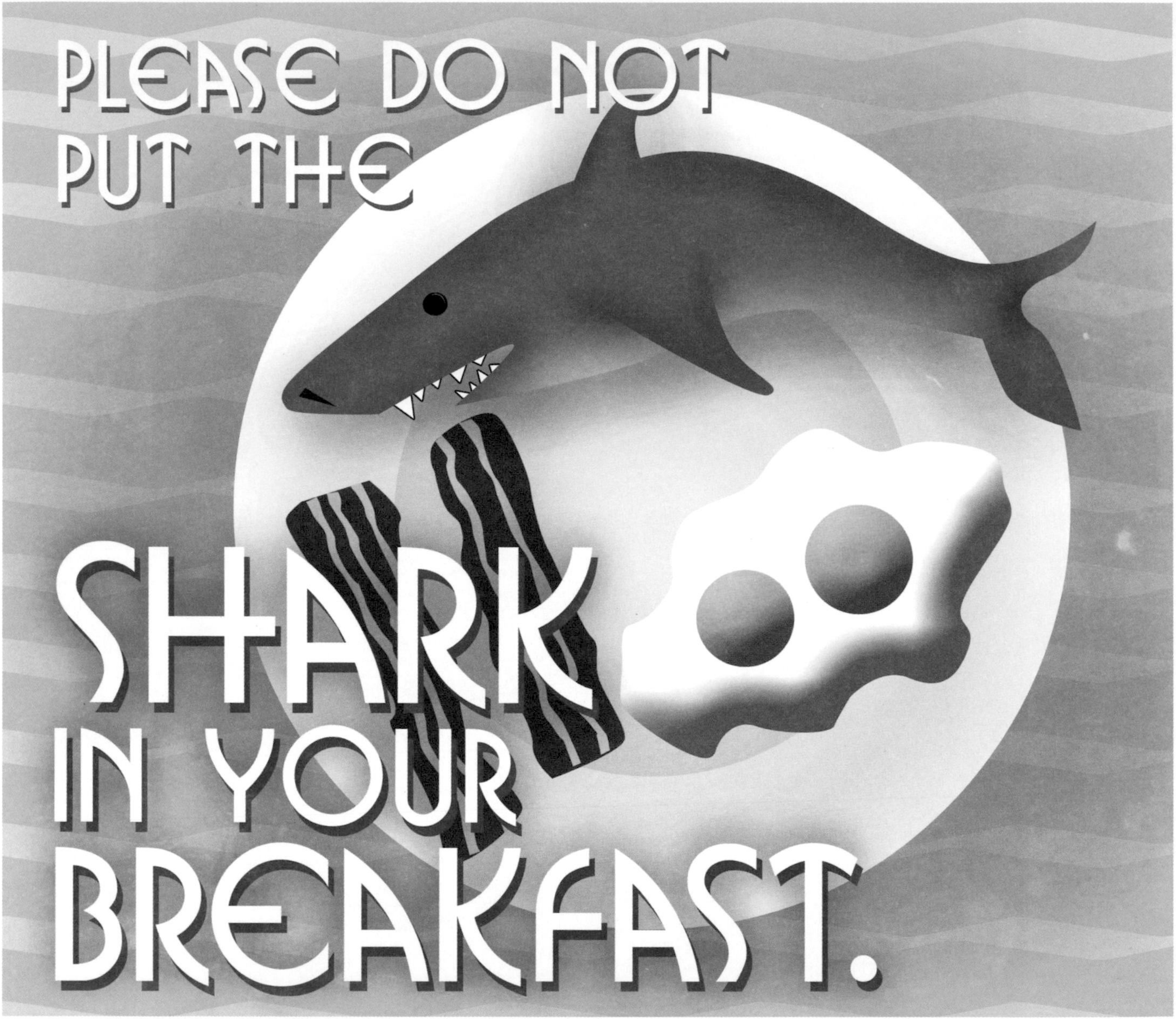
PLEASE DO NOT
PUT THE
SHARK
IN YOUR
BREAKFAST.

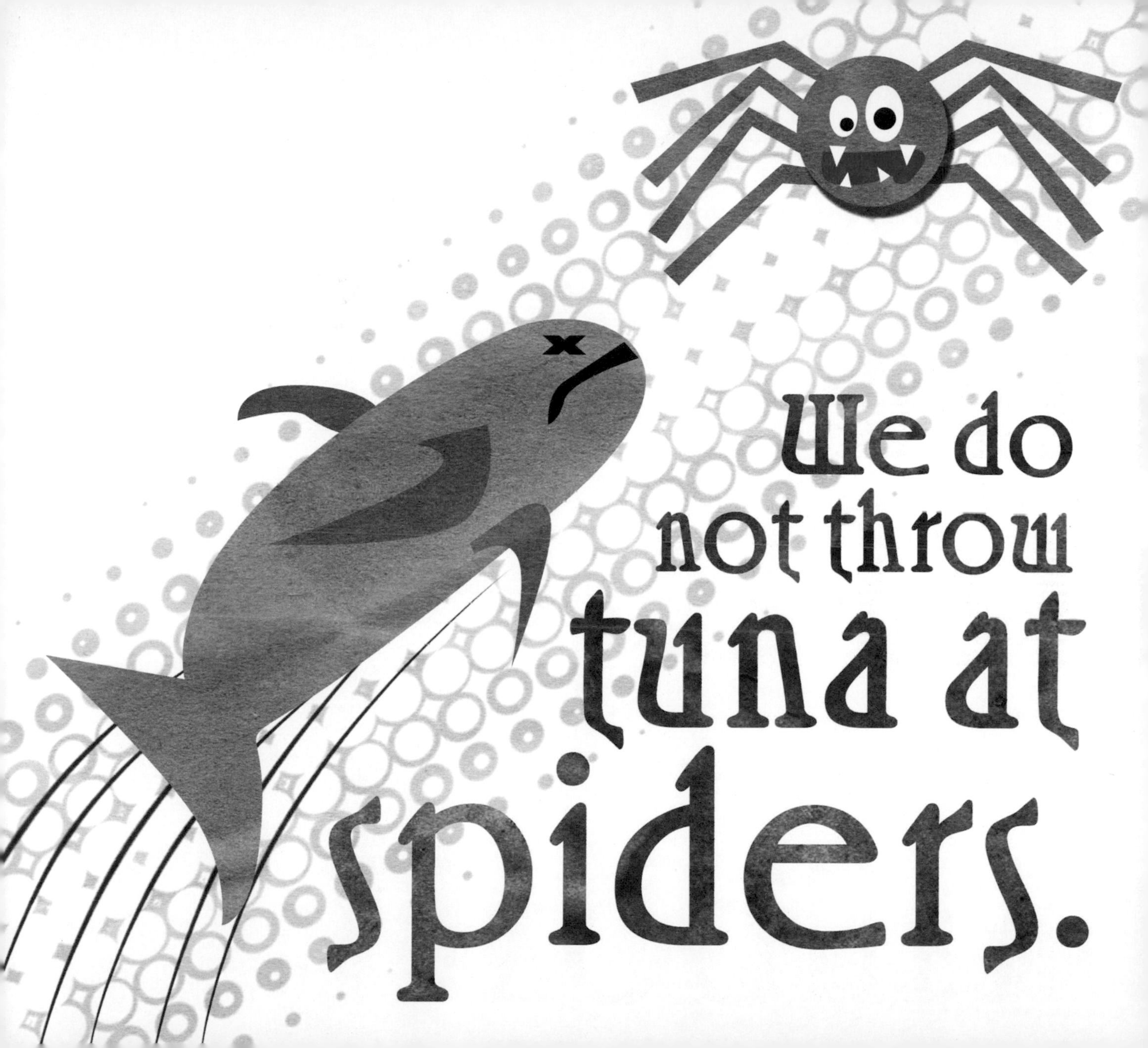

We do not throw tuna at spiders.

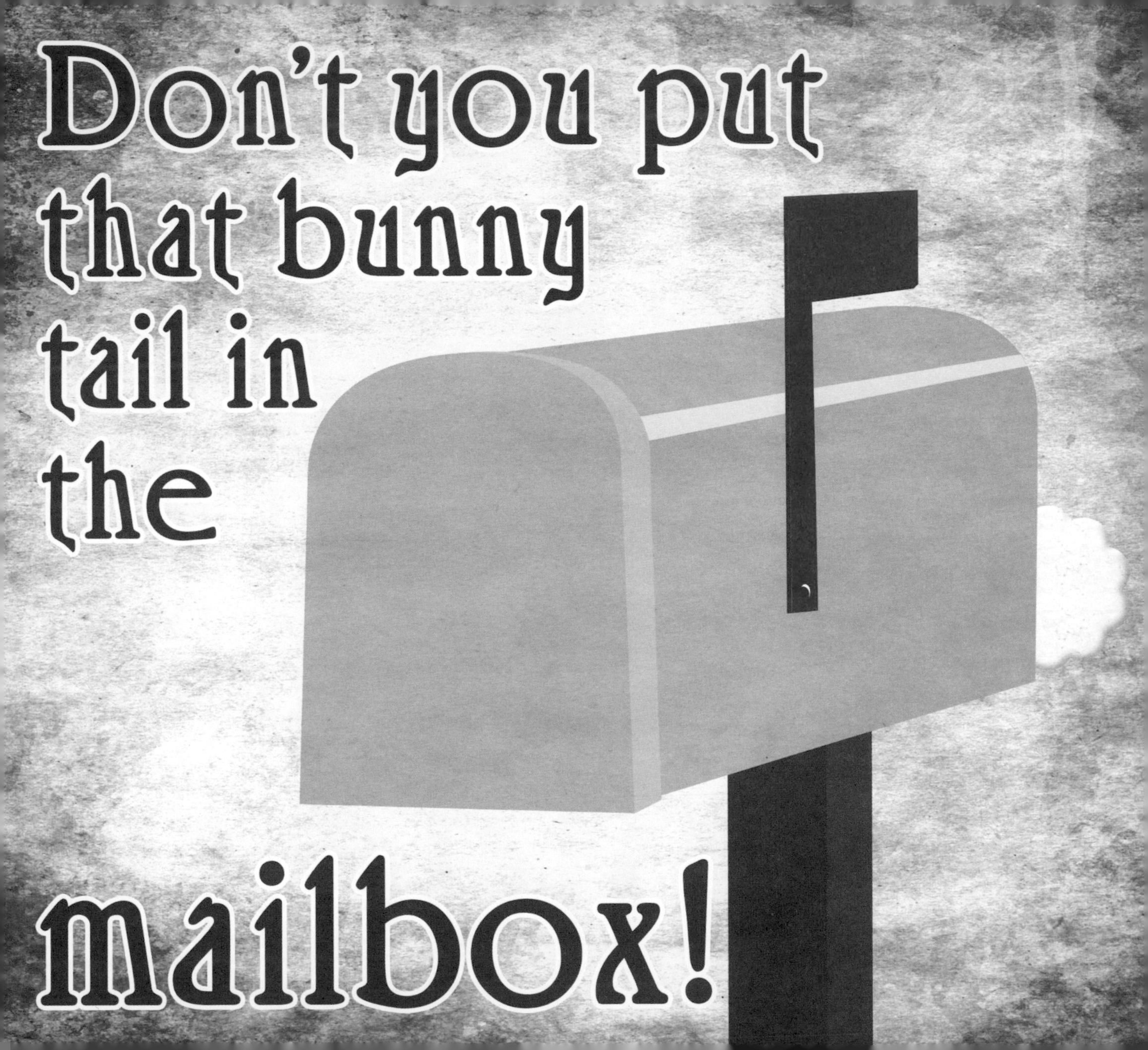
Don’t you put that bunny tail in the mailbox!

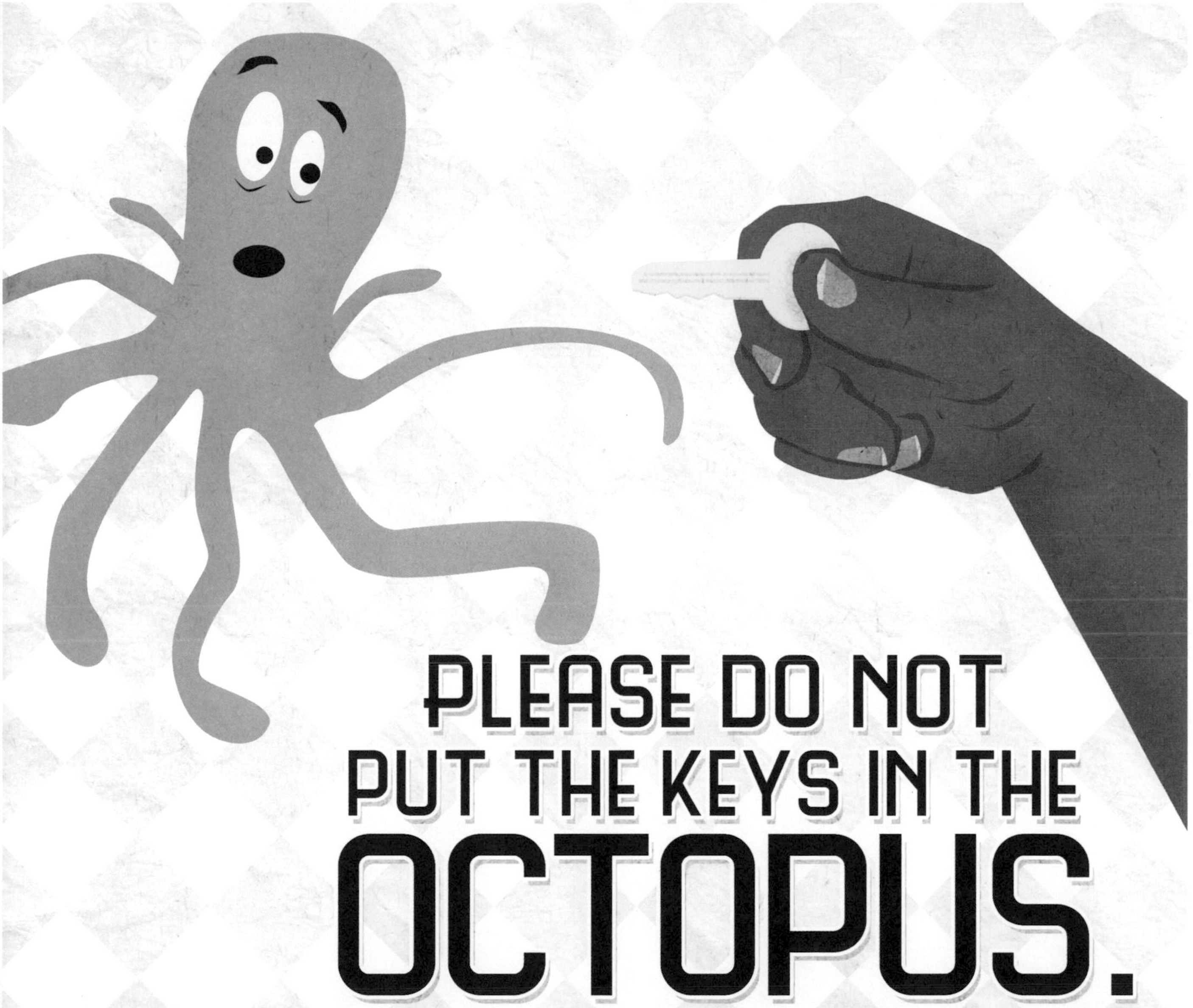
PLEASE DO NOT
PUT THE KEYS IN THE
OCTOPUS.

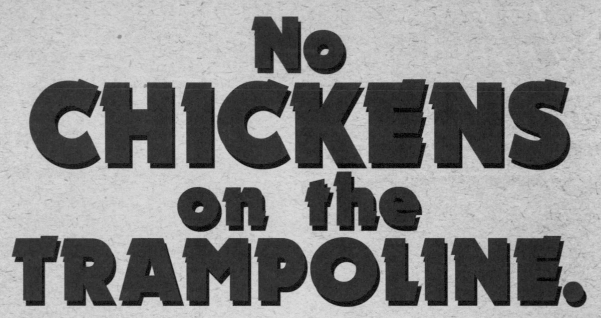

No CHICKENS on the TRAMPOLINE.

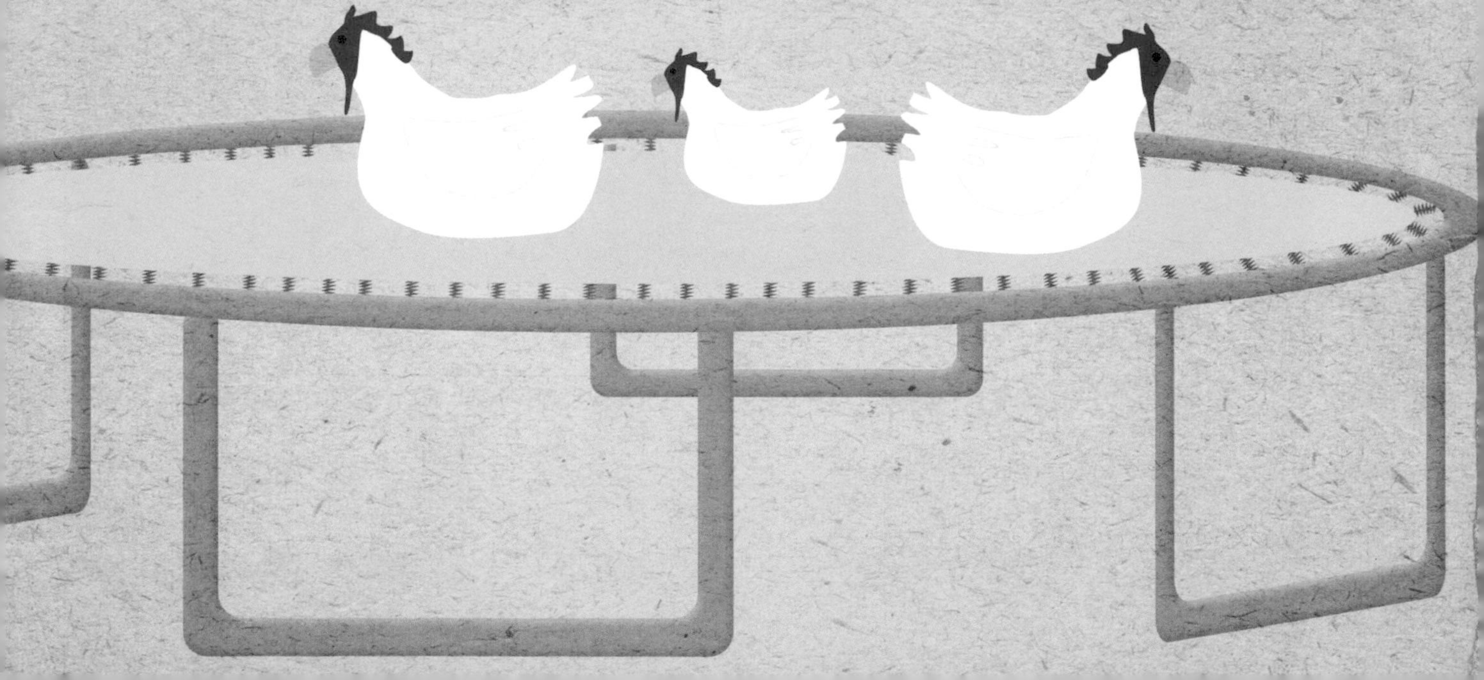